BRIDECHILLA
SURVIVAL GUIDE

BRIDECHILLA

Help grow the Bridechilla movement,
tag a #**BRIDECHILLA** and spread the word!

Join our group the 'Bridechilla Community' on Facebook to meet
like-minded Bridechillas and Groomchillas. It's the best
gosh darn wedding planning community around.

Be sure to follow Bridechilla on
Facebook @thebridechilla
Instagram @bridechilla
Pinterest @bridechillapod

ISBN 9781999916329

Design by Viktoriya Nesheva and Richard Maddock
Illustrations by Robby Satria. Find him on Instagram @obicatlia
Printed in China

First edition 2018, Happy Days Media Inc.
Second edition 2019, Happy Days Media Inc.
Third edition 2020, Happy Days Media Inc.

Happy Days Media Inc. 2020
www.thebridechilla.com

To my first and favorite husband, Rich, whose enthusiasm and support shows no bounds. I love being a member of our team. You make me laugh until I cry. Even though you sometimes wipe your face on the tea towel, every day with you in our tracksuit pants and polar fleeces is a joy.

To all of the Bridechilla Community, you are my people. You've got this.

CONTENTS

Being a Bridechilla is about staying present and positive while saying fuck it to the shouldas, couldas and wouldas.

Bridechilla Katie

Let's Ditch Wedstress

HELLO, I'M ALEISHA. Six years ago I got hitched to Rich. During our wedding planning process, I got really bored with the "plan your perfect day" and the "dream wedding" message. It wasn't us at all. I wanted real information to help us decipher how the hell we were going to put a wedding day together, without going insane or going off-grid until it all blew over. I created *The Bridechilla Podcast* as a way to share all the things I learned during our wedding planning and included all the things I wished we'd known. Since then, thanks to my lovely listeners, it has become the #1 wedding planning podcast and global HQ for the anti–chair cover movement. There is just no need for them, okay?

The podcast is successful because I talk about real wedding stuff. Yes, I share practical details of planning a wedding. But more often than not, I end up sharing the things that mattered to me the most, like relationships and self-esteem. I discuss topics such as the emotional negotiations of wedding planning and how to respond to wedding dress sales assistants called Carol with loose perms who ask, "*How* much weight are you planning to lose?"* I often joke on the podcast that I want to nurture a super army of Bridechillas, people that take it all in stride and don't get stressed or lose their marbles over the little things.

Bridechillas and Groomchillas are strong people who aren't just planning a party – they are finding their voices and doing what's right for them. They emerge on the other side of their wedding feeling empowered and ready to begin their married life knowing what they want out of their relationship. Getting married is a perfect time to clean emotional house, reassess your goals and explore what makes you happy.

This book is for everyone – straight, gay, Millennials, Generation X – and whether this is your first marriage of fourth, I know that you will find value and guidance in these pages. This is the wedding planning book I wanted to read. It's not full of promises of perfection, it's a practical planning guide and relation-ship manifesto. I've combined aesthetic advice about planning a wedding with the questions and topics that so many magazines avoid. There are no rules in Bridechilla– and Groomchilla–land and I encourage you to choose the details that are right for you and ditch the aspects that are not. Being flexible and open to new ideas and ways of doing things will make your wedding planning all the easier and will, no doubt, result in an event that is really you.

When I was trying to get my head around what commitment and balance meant to me, as well as the big decisions surrounding planning a wedding, I felt overwhelmed. So often we only focus on the planning part of it all, we forget to think about why we're doing it and how we're going to keep it all together and growing after the wedding day.

In this guide we will explore the logistics of wedding planning, as well as the emotional decisions and challenges that we face when planning a wedding (like obligation guests, talking about money with your partner and the truth about wedding night sex).

I don't have all the answers. In fact, I'm still figuring out a lot of this stuff my-self. But what I have learned I will share with you.

I hope you enjoy it!

Happy Days
Aleisha x

* The short answer is "Fuck off Carol," but the long answer is about body image and the media and how we've given Carol the power to make us feel so crappy when we should be having an ace time buying our wedding dress.

do what makes you happy, not what makes everyone else happy

Being a Bridechilla means being
authentic in what you want for your
wedding and not crippling yourself
with ridiculously high standards,
price tags and expectations.

Bridechilla Bonnie

Why Are You Getting Hitched?

I'VE BEEN ENGAGED TWICE. Sure, I'm no Elizabeth Taylor (and my first engagement ring went straight on eBay – sayonara bitch), but I can say with the hindsight of experience and age that both engagements couldn't have been further from each other. The big difference was the second engagement ended in a wedding. Winning!

My "original fiancé" (OF) said after watching me perform stand-up comedy I had written about the ordeal of unplanning our wedding, "Surely something more interesting's happened in your life that you can talk about other than our breakup." He's right, there have been heaps of other things that I have experienced in my life, but little did he know that he had entered into a relationship with a budding stand-up comedian. A few years later, partially thanks to this story, I turned it into a profession. He unknowingly gifted me a shitty breakup and a truckload of material that helped me launch my career and brought me to hosting *The Bridechilla Podcast* and writing this book.

In brief, the breakup was a shitshow. We were young. We were each other's first boyfriend and girlfriend and hadn't experienced other serious relationships. Marriage seemed like the next step, something that you did after you'd bought a dog and got a bit bored. I probably bullied him into it in a subconscious way, and he went along with it until he realized that by being engaged and booking a venue and paying money that he was ACTUALLY GETTING MARRIED.

Five weeks before the wedding he had a meltdown, left our home and didn't speak to me for a week. He said he didn't see a future with me and that he might have feelings for a singer in his band. To add to the cliché, he was a guitarist and the singer was a pashmina-wearing Stevie Nicks wannabe. When I approached her to ask about their relationship (oh yes, I went there) she nodded condescendingly and told me about their special connection.

God knows how I didn't punch her in the throat but something calm and very controlled washed over me and I left that encounter feeling like I had been kicked in the guts but also a little free. Fuck them. Fuck her pashminas. If Stevie Nicks had been there, she would have been on my side. I went into survival mode and unplanned the wedding. I called all our vendors, told them my sad story and prayed to the wedding Gods that they would take pity on me and not request full payment so close to the date. Deposits and dignity were lost in those phone calls, but all the vendors, except the venue, were kind and did what they could to help me out.

I was working as a radio producer at the time. After hearing about my predicament with our winery wedding venue, one of the sales managers at the radio station went to bat for me. The venue was asking for full payment (which they were contractually allowed to do). However, the venue was also a big advertiser with the radio station and had neglected to pay their invoices for four months. The sales manager said he'd waive the debt if they waived mine. Job done. I was grateful for the kindness that I received during that time.

I don't have any hard feelings towards the OF. I don't resent the end of the relationship as that was the right decision, but I don't think I can forgive him leaving me to cancel everything on my own. It was a shit move. Selfish. He walked away from any responsibility. He behaved like a child, which summed up the situation perfectly.

I was very aware of avoiding becoming a scorned person. I didn't want to carry the betrayal and hurt from that experience everywhere I went. And yet, just when I thought it was all done and dusted, after stewing for a week, the OF reappeared and tried to patch things up. I was completely blinded by the hope that it had all been some terrible mix-up and that the Stevie Nicks wannabe wasn't waiting in the wings and the ex wasn't just being a huge idiot, coming back to what he knew. We even went on a non-honeymoon and tried to work through it all, but ultimately we were broken and by the end so was I.

More than a decade on I can happily say that when stuff happens, we either learn from it or let it bog us down. In my case, I went a third route. I wrote a stand-up comedy act about it and performed it to rooms of thousands of strangers over and over again. I liked the third option. It was cathartic and cheaper than a psychotherapist.

I'm not sharing my story with you to be a Debbie Downer, but to illustrate my own personal growth. Considering what I thought marriage was about back then and what it means to me now, they are two very different things. Although I wouldn't say I'd love to go through that experience again, it did shape a big chunk of my twenties and who I am today.

The fundamentals of being a Bridechilla are understanding how you feel, knowing what you want, and learning how to communicate it. Listen to the voice that guides your everyday choices. Trust your instinct, that weird tummy feeling that comes when you think you are making a decision that you probably shouldn't. There have been plenty of times in my life when I ignored that feeling, that internal megaphone that says NO, and 99% of the time I should have listened.

I don't believe in fate or fairies. I trust my sense of judgment. The instinct that goes back to caveman times when it acted as a warning saying, "Don't go into that dark part of the woods, you are about to die" or, "Caveman Gary is so sweet to me, but I am suspicious that he is leading me into a cave to club me to death for my bear-hide bolero."

In retrospect, I know in my past relationship I suppressed my ambitions because they weren't supported. The true Aleisha, the person who I am with Rich and my close friends and on the podcast, was suppressed because she wasn't met with smiles. I smothered my enjoyment of hammy pop music, pretending I didn't adore it because he was a "serious musician" and poo-pooed Britney Spears. I missed peak Britney because I wasn't trusting my gut. By shutting down my big ideas and goals, I killed my inner Bridechilla. I strangled her when she could have been twerking to Destiny's Child.

I wasn't me. I didn't know what I wanted because I hadn't allowed myself to imagine it. I had nestled myself in the security of that relationship, the warm cocoon of familiarity that eventually would have closed up and suffocated me. Gosh, so many death analogies – welcome to my wedding planning book! In the end, I am thankful that I got my ass handed to me. Eventually, I allowed myself to heal, flirted with some random dudes, and gave myself a second chance at finding my voice and figuring out what I wanted, something I'm still doing every day.

As a "virtual bridesmaid," I have the privilege of offering to Bridechillas the advice that close friends and family members are sometimes reluctant to give. Often, Bridechillas respond to my advice with, "I needed to hear that," or, "My mom has been telling me that for months but it wasn't until you said it that it hit home." I get it!

Sometimes it takes a stranger or a podcast-host-friend to kick you into gear. Why do you think people share all their stuff on the internet? I've read forum posts revealing intimacies that you know haven't been disclosed elsewhere, but for many there's a comfort in opening up to someone that you will never see again. Dropping some feeling-bombs on the net, letting go of anxiety, asking for advice or sharing odd medical problems brings relief. Getting it off your chest and out in the open and reading that other people are in similar situations to you can be massively reassuring. Our Bridechilla Community on Facebook is a place where you can share your stuff without the bitch judgment of some wedding forums (more on that later).

We live in a time of TMI and sharing fatigue in our online lives. On Facebook and Instagram, we only share one view of reality. We pose for photos fifty times and add filters and only report the good stuff. People unfriend people for being too positive or too whiny (or if you're me you ditch the people who ask friends on Facebook how to fix their appliances or use an air conditioner remote – for fuck's sake, just Google it). The flip side to all of this oversharing is that we can help each other. Perhaps as a community we're not as connected physically as our grandparents were, but we are more honest and open than them, and maybe these annoying screens that we stare at incessantly are the reason for that.

Getting married is a time of renewal. A time when you set up shop with another person, create new traditions, embrace their family as yours and become a team. Use this time to not only focus on planning a wedding, but also planning what you want from your relationships with your partner, family and friends.

We spend so much time focusing on the aesthetics of a wedding, but most of the real stresses of wedding planning come from surrounding issues such as integrating family, how to talk about money and how to suppress unrealistic expectations. Wedding magazines and blogs can be helpful for all of the practical planning advice, but there isn't much chatter about the meaty stuff. The "How do we stay together through ups and downs" stuff or the "Why do we have the same three fights over and over again" stuff.

If I could spend time with Aleisha from the past, the gal who had a penchant for headbands, I would be intrigued to hear what marriage meant to her. I'd like to ask her:

- Why are you getting hitched?
- What does it mean for you?
- Does it provide a sense of security? Is it a confirmation that both of you are in it for the long haul? A symbolic ritual? A fab party?
- Should you be marrying someone who you only present a curated version of yourself to?
- Do you think getting married will provide some magic solution to all of your relationship problems?
- Will being a Mrs make you a proper grown-up?
- Are you happy?
- Why so many headbands?!

I know Aleisha from the past was devastated and embarrassed when she was going through the wedding canceling saga. She survived and eventually became the Aleisha of today. I am grateful for all of the ugly crying to sad music, wondering how I could ever get to know another person like that again. Trying to imagine how I would tell a new person all about the minutiae of my past, my silly stories and explain my headband collection, I felt the weight of the future and the unknown. It was overwhelming.

After a couple of months, I knew I needed a change. I moved to a different city, and into my first share house. I bedded a flatmate and started to write stand-up. I felt alone, but I rose to the challenge and became someone who could see beyond the humiliation of being dumped and having her heart broken, I became a woman who was going to fucking dominate.

I was single for five years, and in that time I had lots of adventures. I lived on my own, had some one night stands (and repeat business), but no real relationships. I had lots of interesting jobs in TV, and just as I was coming to the conclusion that maybe I was going to be a career-focused single stand-up comedian, I met Rich.

Our courtship was fast. We both knew what we wanted and moved in together within months. It was exciting and energizing. Our relationship was everything I wanted and never had before. When I consider questions about the meaning of marriage, I know my answers now are completely different to past Aleisha's answers.

Why are you getting hitched?
- We're a team and we love each other.
- We want to share our commitment to each other with our family and friends.
- We want to have a kick ass party.

Will being a Mrs make you a proper grown-up?
- No. I may never fully grow up, and I am fine with that. Adulting is boring.

Are you happy?
- Between waves of crippling existential dread, yes.

Why so many headbands?
- I thought they were sophisticated, but they just made me look like a twelve-year-old.

These answers will not only help you move forward with a clear view of what you want for your future (with your partner and yourself), but they will also help you level up when it comes to planning your wedding day. Communication and honesty will get you a long way in this gig. If you can talk about money and expectations, what will make you both happy, why certain things are non-negotiables for you and if you learn the sometimes very delicate act of compromise, then you will be all the better for it. I have so much to share I am bursting, and I promise I won't speak in the third person again.

BRIDECHILLA STEPS

> **Take a moment to reflect on how you think marriage might change your relationship (if at all).**
> **Work through the marriage questions – did any of your or your partner's answers surprise you?**
> **Talk openly with your partner about your expectations and hesitations about wedding planning and beyond.**

if you stumble, make it
part of the dance

Being a Bridechilla means knowing
what you want and going for it
with gusto – while understanding,
respecting and supporting another
bride's completely different choices.

Bridechilla Nichole

Questions to Ask Each Other Before Saying I Do

WHETHER YOU HAVE BEEN IN A RELATIONSHIP with your partner for six months or six years, taking the time to go through the questions on this list as a pre-wedding deep dive will help you know where you both stand on life views, long- and short-term goals and things that you should know about each other.

There are no right answers. You don't have to agree with each other – in fact it's good to have differing opinions on things because that's what makes us who we are! Saying that, if there are big questions like, "Do you want to have kids?" that you do have differing views on, then this is a good time to work together to get on the same page or at least understand each other's perspectives and work together to find a balance.

THINGS WE DON'T TALK ABOUT AT DINNER PARTIES

- Are you an optimist or a pessimist?
- What are your religious views?
- What are your political views?
- How important is spending time alone to you?
- Would you lie to me to protect my feelings?
- What does being married mean to you?
- Where do you see your career in the future?
- Is there anything you don't trust about me?
- What are your views on abortion and birth control?
- What is your process of making big decisions?
- If I became disabled or incapacitated, would you look after me?
- What would you do if someone said something bad about me?
- Would you follow the advice of your family over the advice of your spouse?

- What do you believe the role of a wife is?
- What do you believe the role of a husband is?
- Who should do household chores?

NEW LIFE

- Do you want to have children?
- If you do, how many children do you imagine us having?
- What values do you wish to pass on to our children?
- Do you have a family history of diseases or genetic abnormalities?
- How far apart in age do you want children to be?
- What if our children didn't want to go to college?
- How comfortable are you around children?
- How do you believe we will handle parental decisions?
- Would you be opposed to having our parents watch the children so we can spend time alone together?
- What sort of education do you envisage our children having?
- What are your thoughts on home schooling?
- Would you want to adopt if we couldn't have kids?
- Would you consider seeking medical intervention if we couldn't conceive naturally?
- How would you want to discipline our kids?
- Do you believe it's okay to discipline children in public?
- How do you feel about paying for your children's college education?
- Would you want someone to stay home with the kids or use day care?
- How would you feel if our kids wanted to join the military rather than go to college?
- How involved do you want grandparents to be in our parenting?

EXTENDED FAMILY

- If one of your family said they disliked me, would that affect how you feel about me?
- If your parents became ill, could they live with us?
- If my parents became ill, could they live with us?
- How often would you want to visit your family?
- How often will your family visit us?
- How often would you want my family to visit?
- How often would you want to visit my family?
- Where and with whom do you want to spend the holidays?

RELATIONSHIP

- What is your biggest fear about marriage?
- What excites you about getting married?
- Will you wear a wedding ring?
- Are you afraid to talk to me about anything?
- How can I work to better communicate with you?
- Are you open to relationship/marriage counseling?
- How do you handle disagreements?
- Where do you want to live?
- What are your career aspirations?
- Would you mind moving if I had to relocate with my job?
- What would you do if we fell out of love?
- What would you like to be doing five or ten years from now?
- What do you think is the best way to keep the love alive in a marriage?
- How do you think life will change if we got married?
- What is the best thing about marriage?
- What is the worst thing about marriage?
- What is your idea of the best weekend?
- How important are wedding anniversaries to you?
- How would you like to spend special days?
- What type of house do you want to live in?
- Would you like to build a house one day?
- What do you think would improve our relationship?
- What would be one thing you would change about our relationship?
- Do you have any doubts about the future of our relationship?
- Do you believe love can pull you through anything?
- If there is a disagreement between your spouse and your family, whose side would you choose?
- Would you ever consider divorce?
- Have you ever cheated on a partner or been cheated on?
- Are you comfortable with discussing your issues?
- If you aren't satisfied sexually in our relationship would you tell me?
- What is the best way to handle disagreements in a marriage?

MONEY

- Do you have any debt?
- How do you feel about having a joint bank account?

- What are your views on saving money?
- What are your views on spending money?
- What if we both want something but can't afford both things?
- Have you ever created and stuck to a budget?
- Do you have investments? Shares? Bitcoin?
- Do you feel it is important to save for retirement?
- Would you be willing to get a second job if we had financial problems?
- What would you do if a family member wants to borrow a large sum of money?
- Should we share financial responsibilities, such as paying bills?

THE GREAT ESCAPE

- Do you enjoy traveling?
- Are you a hotel or hostel type of traveler?
- Where would you like to travel to?
- How important is spending time with friends (without me) to you?
- What would be the ideal weekday evening to you?
- What inspires you to travel?
- How often would you like to take a holiday?
- Do you prefer relaxing holidays, or are you an adventure seeker?

HEALTH

- What is your family medical history?
- Does anyone in your family suffer from alcoholism/drug addiction?
- Have you ever felt depressed or suffered from mental illness?
- Are you on any medications?
- If I had to change my diet due to a medical condition, would you be willing to change yours?
- Are you willing to exercise with me to improve our health?

MISCELLANEOUS

- Washing up or drying?
- Do you like pets?
- What do you want to do during retirement?
- If you can't find the TV remote, would you blame me?
- If I was a zombie in the apocalypse, would you put me down?
- If I murdered someone, would you tell the cops?

there are no wrong answers

A Bridechilla is someone who, despite all the details, knows that if by the end of her wedding day she is married then the day is a success.

Bridechilla Alana

The Wedding Industry

What you need to know

WHEN ARE YOU GETTING MARRIED? What dress are you wearing? What time will the ceremony start? Will you serve Sauvignon Blanc or Chardonnay? Will it be a religious service? Can I bring a date? When will you be sending invitations? Are you having a gift registry? You call yourself an atheist, but will you still be getting married in a church? Will there be a band? Are you wearing white?

These are just some of the questions asked within the first sixty seconds of announcing your engagement. Why do they do that? Logic says they know that you don't have the answers. You just got engaged. When would you have had time to lock all that shit down? Relax, Aunty Val. We'll tell you when we've had three freaking minutes to think about it, 'kay?

Aside from committing yourself to another person forever (OK, half of you – sorry, I'm a realist), you've also signed up to organizing potentially the most expensive party of your life. When we break it down, that's what a wedding is. It's a really fabulous, but rather expensive, party. We've all heard the crazy stats about the cost of weddings that are rolled out every year: "On average, couples spend between $25,000 and $40,000 on a wedding." I call bullshit.

These numbers may be true for some areas (like London, NYC or Sydney) and I don't doubt that a bunch of people do spend that much on their wedding day, but not everyone does. Although I don't want to invoke the Wedding Illuminati, it does seem to me that these figures are a convenient device to make people think that they have to spend that sort of money; that it's normal. When you delve a little deeper into the companies who create these annual spending surveys, it's a smart move. They rely on advertising revenue from businesses who charge higher prices for their stuff. It's good for them to promote these averages and pump up the pressure and normalization of prices. But after all the hype, where does it leave most of us who aren't royalty or who don't have access (or the desire) to blow that sort of cash on a party? Some couples stretch their friendship with credit cards and the bank of Mom and Dad. I am regularly contacted by PR companies representing banks, wanting me to share their "Fantastic new low-interest wedding loan," offers that I politely decline saying, "Have you listened to my show!? Please shove it up your ass".

It's crazy that in the last twenty years the wedding industry has, for most of us, turned a relatively sensible occasion into something bordering on insane. Attitudes have changed, Pinterest was invented, and somehow we ended up here, at the point of ordinary folk dropping $50,000 on a wedding.

DITCHING THE CONCEPT OF PERFECTION

The other thing you are going to see and read a lot are the phrases "dream wedding day," "best day of your life," "perfect day," and the "happiest day of your life." You'll soon find that the wedding industry is brimming with these messages. It's our time to feel special. We should feel like a princess. This is your one moment, but if you miss it, it will most likely never happen again — and if it does, you shouldn't enjoy it as much because you failed the first time. This is our peak happiness. Everything must be Instagram-able and meet the guidelines of a dreamy Style Me Pretty submission. Smiling brides with luscious, full braids and flower crowns greet us on newsstands and as soon as we change our relationship status to "engaged" on Facebook, we become the prime target for weight loss advertisements and teeth whitening trays. The Greek chorus of be better, look better and spend more money is overwhelming. The concepts of the "best day of your life" and planning a "perfect day" are thrown around like they are attainable.

The day I married my husband Rich was fabulous, but I hope for both of our sakes we have a bunch more "best days of our lives." I didn't want the wedding to be the peak of our existence and everything after to be a downward trajectory. I'm not anti-consumer. I love buying stuff, probably a little too much, but I do get quite tetchy when I think about the consumerist pressure put on couples to buy a bunch of shit they don't need. The industry pushes the idea that the more stuff you buy and the more "unique" you strive to make your wedding, the more fun and memorable it will be.

There is no denying that champagne and quality canapés are lovely additions to the day, and that being in a gorgeous venue with a band playing your favorite tunes making you want to shake your ass is great. But thinking back on the weddings that we have attended that have felt magical — well, the magic had nothing to do with the napkins and doughnut walls. Guess what did make them special?

The drugs. Just kidding. It was the people. The feeling. The love. The realness of it all. I think we've all been to a wedding where the couple has shelled out a bunch of cash, and you watch their ceremony with a level of numbness. You don't feel the love (even if it's there) and you shuffle into a swanky hotel lobby to eat some appetizers and smash some cocktails, and then you move into the big ballroom to eat more and dance to a band that looks good but has no soul. The event itself is good on paper, but without personality and authenticity, it's just a big event.

BRIDEZILLA = BULLSHIT

The term Bridezilla is a piece of shit. I didn't invent the term Bridechilla, but I have made it our own. In the olden days, before the 2004 reality show and subsequent inclusion in our everyday vernacular, a Bridezilla was just known as a stressed-out bride. Now, Bridezillas have evolved into a neat stereotype, an out-of-control woman, unwilling to compromise to reach her ambition of having a so-called "perfect day."

For the uninitiated, planning a wedding can be a pretty intense experience, and for many couples it can feel like they're taking on second full-time jobs. There are seemingly thousands of options and decisions to make. Gone are the days when your mom helped plan a four-hour buffet and dance at the local golf club. Modern weddings, even deceptively simple, intimate affairs, have evolved into epic productions, inspired by the bazillion images of styled shoots and weddings with budgets bigger than the GDP of Botswana featured on Pinterest and Instagram.

The reality show *Bridezillas* painted the intensity of wedding planning in a pretty grim light. Following women who were determined to realize their "dream wedding" at all costs, it was car crash TV at its best – and worst. The Bridezillas were presented as out-of-control humans, who were determined to have the "best day of their lives," while those around them cowered and cringed, questioning how much time off the friendship they might need after the wedding before they could face them again. The show, like so many after it, followed a successful, repeated formula of find the extreme and push it to the limit. Watch them crack, repeat, repeat, repeat. It was all fun and games until the term Bridezilla became the go-to insult for any bride who was struggling with the pressure and the palaver that can occur while planning a wedding.

I feel that fundamentally most Bridezillas are women who feel completely overwhelmed and unsupported while planning this often-complicated event (granted, some people are just dicks though, and I shall not defend them for being that way). For many couples, weddings come with emotional and financial baggage made up of complicated family relationships, mental health issues, money pressures, expectations and obligations. All of these factors can lead to *wedstress*, an extreme anxiety surrounding wedding planning. People deal with stress in different ways. Some grind their teeth (me!), some sulk and some act out, especially towards those closest to them who are quick to forgive and move on.

Bridechillas are concerned about relationships and the pressure to do things a certain way. They're modern people who are conflicted by ditching tradition. They are keen to forge a path, create an event that reflects them and what their love means, but are fearful of not living up to the expectations of those around them and on the internet.

For many, wedstress begins before there's even talk of a ring, with 70% of today's brides pinning to wedding Pinterest boards before they are even engaged. The consumer wedding industry is now worth billions. Each year a new survey run by an advertising funded wedding magazine reminds us about the exorbitant average costs of weddings...and on the very next page encourages us to purchase an $8,000 wedding dress.

Take time to step back and remember that ultimately it's your relationship that you're celebrating, not bunting and colored smoke bombs and donut walls (although they are my new favorite fad...mmmmm...donuts). Remember that you are one of the lucky ones who have found your fellow weirdo, the love of your life and someone who finds you sexy even if you wear a night retainer to prevent teeth grinding (me again!).

The Bridezilla is a construct, an invention of reality TV that has been embraced by the masses. The term shoehorns women with an opinion, women who are stressed and women who feel overwhelmed into one label – like we need any more of those! The confusing messages of the wedding industry, the Pinterest boards and the pressure to keep up with the Joneses can make everyone (men included) feel like their wedding is the be-all and end-all of their lives.

Weddings are great, but I sincerely hope we can shift perspective, ditch the cliché and labels, and encourage couples to spend a little more time supporting each other and planning what comes after the wedding, because with all hope there are plenty more "best days" to come.

PEOPLE-PLEASING 101

I am a people-pleaser. I am overly polite (if that's a thing) and worry far too much about what people think of me and how my actions may affect them. This statement may come as a surprise to some of my *Bridechilla* listeners, as I know the zero fucks attitude that I convey on the show is the driving force of the whole Bridechilla movement. This is all true. I am strong and opinionated, but one of my areas of personal improvement is working on ways to ditch my need to please and my sensitivity surrounding other people's feelings. Having the ability to read situations can be great, being socially perceptive is a skill that a lot of people lack and some people just don't give a shit about at all (which sucks). Being a people-pleaser can be conflicting, especially when you are an independent, sassy broad. I know that it is not possible to make everyone happy all of the time, but still I strive to make it that way, which is the bane of every people-pleaser's life.

I understand where my people-pleasing desires began. Moments of instability in my childhood caused me to change behavior and adapt, probably far earlier than any child should have to learn those skills. As an adult, I know the consequences of that experience have been both positive and negative. I have a very strong work ethic, I am very determined and independent, but on the other hand, I know I am probably too sensitive to other people's behavior and reactions. I take things on board and make it a personal mission to try and help and fix situations. Rich always says, "You can't save everyone," and although I get what he means, I'm certainly no martyr. I just like to keep the peace.

It's taken me a long time to understand and come to terms with the fact that my actions may not always be accepted with open arms by everyone in my life, but that doesn't mean my actions are wrong and it doesn't mean they're not in my best interest. People-pleasing for many Bridechillas is a natural state and it can be a real challenge to change your behavior when planning your wedding. When you have people placing their expectations on you, even if those expectations are unrealistic or not what you want, it can be really hard to ignore those requests and not feel bad. Of course, every situation is unique, but before you jump into people-pleasing mode I ask you to take a breath. Instead of moving to do what you think will make someone else happy or make the situation easier, pause a minute.

I ask you to consider what's right for you, even if the prospect of challenging someone's opinion or suggestion makes you feel uncomfortable or awkward. Take that step to do something that's right for you. Finding your voice isn't always easy, but once you do, it will be a defining moment that will help shape the steps that you take in the future. Shedding some of the people-pleasing attributes doesn't mean that you have to be unkind or unthoughtful. In a way it's the complete opposite because you are listening to yourself, your desires and your needs which, for people who give so much, is often the last thing that we choose to do. Be strong, and do the right thing for you.

BRIDECHILLA STEPS

> **Understand that the wedding industry and their messages are not always in your best interest – be open but be aware!**
> **Be inspired by Pinterest and Instagram, but don't allow them to be the driving force in your planning.**

A Bridechilla doesn't take herself too seriously! This is an important day, but also, like, it's a DAY. Do what you can and make it what you want, but know that people will enjoy it no matter what and they are there to celebrate you. It's a celebration, not the fucking culmination of your life!

Bridechilla Taylor

Your Money Story

EVERYONE'S ATTITUDES TOWARD MONEY ARE DIFFERENT, we all have our own money story. Your money story is made up of a lifetime of your collected observations of funds and finance. Many of your money values probably come from your parents and extended family's attitudes about spending and saving, experiencing financial hardship, highs and lows, good times and bad. From childhood, we absorb reactions and attitudes toward money, whether they are "good" or "bad."

On a simple level, how much exposure you had to these experiences and the understanding and processing of this information created your adult money story. When we read statistics that the most common fight couples have is money-related, it's easy to understand why. With so many differing money stories floating about, how can everyone agree on how to spend and save in a new union?

My money story is very different from my husband Rich's. One of my earliest money memories was when I was around 7, accompanying my mother to an ATM. My parents divorced when I was very young, and at the time I was living with my mother. On this occasion, I recall watching Mom having a meltdown because the money she thought would be there wasn't. As a single parent, money was tight, and my mother would keep me up-to-date on the level of deep financial shit that we were in. I remember being worried. I was seven and worried about money. I felt helpless and jealous of "normal families" that could afford to go on holidays and friends that had Commodore 64 computers and Fido Dido T-shirts. I wanted all that stuff, but mostly I wanted my mother to stop talking about not having any money.

My mother wasn't frivolous, but she wasn't mindful of her money either. She was a dreamer and always maintained that things would get better, although I am not sure she ever had any plans in motion for change. When I was 10, my mother became sick, so I went to live with my Dad. It was the early 1990s, and Australia was just coming out of one of the most brutal recessions in history. Work came and went and there was a lot of uncertainty around, but Dad worked hard.

One day Dad surprised me by taking a sunglasses case from his sock drawer. When he opened it, it was full of cash. I'm not talking Walter White money here, but it was certainly a few thousand dollars.

"We're going skiing!" he declared, and we did, and it was awesome.

I don't know how long he was saving money and adding to that case. That magic moment of seeing wads of notes was the complete opposite of my mother's ATM meltdown, but it affected me in a similar way. Money appeared and disappeared. We either had none or a bit. There was no consistency. There were plenty of times that my Dad didn't have a sunglasses case of cash to save the day. He had very different values and expectations about money than my mother. My Dad is a hard worker, believes in saving up and buying quality items that will last a long time. He thinks credit cards are trouble.

My mother was a dreamer and perhaps overly optimistic about where future money was coming from. She was skilled at upping and leaving when times got tough and had Madonna-like reinvention skills. Breaking it down in this way makes my personal money story crystal clear.

By the time I was 16, I had gotten my first summer job at a homewares store and pretty much from then on I have been financially independent. I valued every cent that I earned in that job and was careful with how I spent it. I got my first credit card at the age of 24 and gave it a solid workout. I made payments but rarely cleared it to 0. I chose life experiences over stability and saving (especially after my big breakup with OF). I worked contract gigs, money came and went. I purchased quality over crap; I traveled, I enjoyed, I worked hard. Rinse and repeat.

When I met Rich, I realized that we shared a similar urge to travel and invest in experiences over stuff, but I also learned that he came from a much more stable money story. His parents were still together and lived in the same house that he was born in (and his Dad was born in), he'd been privately educated, and he wasn't a believer in credit cards. He was a saver. If it wasn't in the account, you didn't spend it.

In the early days of a relationship, most people overlook bumps in merging their money stories together because they're too busy having sex and forgetting about reality. As the relationship grows you start doing sensible things like buying furniture and paying bills. This is usually where the cracks in the money stories are revealed, and disagreements begin to happen.

For us, our first money argument as a couple was about holidays (and in some ways from time to time we still have a different version of the same argument). I wanted to go on a holiday and Rich wanted us to work together to pay off the credit card (my debt) so we could start afresh in our new life together. Of course, now I see that Rich just wanted to get rid of the STD (Sexually Transmitted Debt) that I had given him.

His wanting to clear the deck of my debt was perfectly reasonable and generous! At the time I had connected a sense of shame to that debt and felt awful that my past was preventing us from lying on a beach in Thailand sipping cocktails.

Why should we, as a couple, suffer from my bad money management? In the end, we came to a compromise. We worked our butts off to clear and cut up the credit cards and when it was done, we booked a cheapo package tour for a week in Phuket to celebrate. I also paid off my student loans and felt a weight lift off my shoulders.

Our money stories are ingrained in us. Often they're unchangeable, or at least hard to budge. However, understanding where the other person's financial beliefs and understandings come from and trying to understand why they act a certain way with their cash can help you be a better team. If you haven't had these conversations before getting engaged, no problem – you can do it now! It is never too late to learn more about your partner and what makes them tick. It's also never too late to talk about STDs. Old debts from past relationships shouldn't be the stuff of shame, but if you don't talk about them, acknowledge them, and plan to eradicate them, then it can create challenges that you could otherwise avoid.

If you are on the same page, or at least understand each other's thought processes around money and what you value, that understanding can be the foundations for a strong team and it will make things so much easier when the wedding planning budget questions start rolling in.

BRIDECHILLA STEPS: ASK EACH OTHER THESE QUESTIONS

> **What's your money story?**
> **What's your earliest money memory?**
> **Did your parents talk about money?**
> **Did you have a lot or a little?**
> **Were you comfortable (even if perhaps your parents weren't)?**
> **What do you value when it comes to money?**
> **What are your money goals?**
> **Have you ever been in debt?**
> **If you argue about money what is the fight about? Your spending? Their spending? Saving? Future plans?**
> **How can you both work together to change your money perspective and create a new money story?**

A Bridechilla is someone who has, with their partner, identified what is important to them for their wedding, and goes about doing it, while intentionally choosing NOT to invest time, money, or emotional energy in aspects of weddings they do not care about or traditions they do not wish to participate in or include.

Wedding Planner Cindy Savage

Wedding Budget

What do you both want and how much is it going to cost?

WITHOUT MONEY, YOUR WEDDING CELEBRATIONS MAY BE SPARSE. Your wedding budget, the money that you will use to pay for all the nice things – alcohol, donut walls, cute shoes – and important things – celebrant, venue, cake – is a vital figure in guiding the decisions you will make for your wedding day. We often feel inclined to make these decisions quickly. We get excited and jump in before we're ready. When are you getting married? Where are you getting married? How many people will you invite? How much will it cost? Where will you get the money to pay for it all? Who are your bridesmaids? Will your wedding dress search be featured on *Say Yes To The Dress*, where you will inevitably end up committing to a dress that is $7000 over your budget because it's "the one"? Here are three things to do before you buy that jumbo wedding planning folder and start organizing.

BASK IN IT

There is something rather wonderful about enjoying the moment. Take it all in. How often do you get engaged? (Don't answer that!) Perhaps you were surprised by the proposal, or maybe you proposed to each other or maybe it had been planned for years. Either way, the engagement period, the time before you both become wedding planning machines, is a time to enjoy and celebrate. Sure, buy a few magazines and listen to a wedding planning podcast or two, but allow yourself the wonderful feeling of anticipation and let the joy of the moment sink in. Drink champagne, eat cake, let people be happy for you and celebrate. A lot. Milk that shit.

BE HONEST

Before you make any plans, get any quotes, call any form of expert, or even dare to open a calendar, I'm going to need you to sit down with your partner and have a proper chat about your expectations for your wedding day and, more importantly, your marriage. Not to get too heavy, but a wedding is, with any luck, an introduction to a long and happy life together. A love merger. A team maker! What do you both want? What do you call a successful marriage?

This may seem obvious but have you told each other? Have you thought about it? If your answer is "not getting divorced" – do not pass go, do not collect $200, go straight to jail. Starting the journey off together on the same path will make things a hell of a lot easier later on, and I'm not just talking about weddings.

We have some close friends who didn't seriously have the "kid chat" until a couple of years into their marriage. He assumed that having a baby was in their future. She didn't want kids. They'd talked about it in passing, and he thought that she'd come around. That it was a phase and as they got deeper into their relationship and more committed, that she'd change her mind.

She did not.

It was an awful deal breaker for both of them and devastating to watch their relationship untangle because they wanted different things.

I am not suggesting you need to make a five-year plan or to map stuff out in spreadsheets, but being able to communicate your expectations about your life together is something that will make you stronger and more aware of the needs and wants of the other person you are committing to be with.

If you were to sit down now in a mock exam, could you say what sort of wedding your partner would like to have?

- What is their ideal budget?
- Who is on their guest list?
- What are their music choices?
- Would they consider an elopement or destination wedding perhaps?

Maybe you envisage a wedding week extravaganza with 300 guests and multiple events and parties, but your partner always imagined getting hitched in a bookshop with 12 people.

Perhaps you imagine eloping, escaping to a tropical destination, where you can get married barefoot on a beach, but your partner was hoping to have a big, formal black-tie event with canapés and everyone wearing shoes!

Having an open discussion and hearing each other's thoughts and opinions early on before you spend any money or make any commitments will ensure you are both celebrating at the same event.

There is a lot of bias in the wedding industry, pushing that it is just a one-sided day, that women are the only people interested in planning weddings and that men are really only showing up on the day and deciding which liquor to serve and perhaps dabbling in the playlist. There seems to be a lopsided projection of priorities that is perpetuated over and over again. This is your day. Two people coming together. I say, start the planning just as you will end your wedding day – as a team. Here are some basic questions to get you started:

- What are both of your non-negotiables when it comes to the day? Good photography? Perhaps you don't care for flowers but want an amazing band to get the dance floor pumping?
- What are the three elements that are important to you? Atmosphere? Food? Fantastic music?
- What do you think is a reasonable figure to spend on planning your wedding?
- How can you use your budget to create an event that will be memorable without having to miss out on things or go into debt?

If you're both on the same page (and I don't mean you have to have all the answers right now), you can start the process off as a team – which is what you are!

WHAT'S YOUR WEDDING FIGURE?

After you've had your chat about expectations, it's time to drill down and think about money. How much have you got and how much do you want to spend? I am talking real figures here, not "If we won the lottery," or "If we sold a kidney each," or "If I do an extra forty-six shifts at work." I mean what is the real figure that you can afford without going into debt or seeking the services of a loan shark?

No matter what your final budget is, the quickest way to get a handle on costs is to be honest with yourself about what you can spend. Not what you'd like to spend, but what is realistic. Being truthful about your budget isn't saying you have to give up on what you want, it's just the first Bridechilla step in deciding what is important to you for the day and what you can cut back on and get creative with.

I used to live in a bit of a money dreamland. A land where something marvellous was always going to come along and save my ass: a money tree, a spot on *Deal Or No Deal* (yep, I was actually a contestant and won $5,000), a long-lost dead relative that would leave me a country estate and shares in Apple that they purchased in 1984. I wasn't irresponsible; I just wasn't aware. In my late twenties, I woke up from my money haze and decided to stop being a debt slave who got palpitations every time the credit card bill arrived.

When we got engaged, Rich and I set up a new savings account. We decided that $10,000 was the absolute maximum we could afford to spend on our wedding. Sure, we could have saved up and spent more, but when it came down to it, we did not want to get a loan and give up holidays and dinners out for the next five years. We had a year to save and organize and thought $10,000 was realistic.

When you have decided on your final budget, set that as a cap and do your best to not go over it. The easiest way to do that is to separate wedding money and everyday money. If your budget is $15,000, create a wedding bank account and only pay for wedding costs from that account. Don't dip into your everyday money. It's easy to spend a bit here, a bit there and blow the budget completely. There are a plethora of online savings accounts that are free and convenient for keeping track of spending online.

Go back to your non-negotiables. When you imagine your wedding, what do you see? Is it a big, lavish party? Is it a cultural celebration? Is it about great food and wine? What would you exchange or let go of to make this day match your expectations? For example, if your "dream" dress were $6,000 and your total wedding budget were $10,000, then either the reception is going to be pretty sparse, or you need to pick another dress. There are big decisions, and it's only the beginning.

If your future husband/wife doesn't seem as enthralled by the details of the day, get them involved. If they don't seem jazzed about the turquoise and pink color scheme, it might be because they secretly loathe it. Or maybe they don't give a shit about color schemes but really care about the music. You won't know if you don't ask.

TAKE NOTE

Create a notebook, download an app to collect quotes, and keep track of receipts. Record all costs, no matter how big or small that are incurred when planning the wedding to create an accurate record of spending. The *Bridechilla Field Guide* is perfect for this – visit bridechillastore.com to order your copy.

A budget can only be kept when you're honest and organized. As an inspirational quote I read on Instagram while in the restroom once said, "It's the honesty system, and you're only cheating yourself."

Planning a wedding should be memorable, special, and fun, but it shouldn't be the be-all and end-all of your existence. Bridechillas and Groomchillas, planning your wedding will be awesome because you are going to figure out exactly what is meaningful to you when it comes to your wedding day and that will make things so much easier. You will deflect the bullshit and just like Fleetwood Mac advises, go your own way.

Rich and I pretty much stuck to our wedding budget. We didn't long for anything, and few sacrifices were made, but we did use up a lot (A LOT) of our own time, energy, and effort making it happen – but that's not everyone's bag.

The benefit of hindsight has made me realize that for a little extra money we could have hired a wedding planner (more on that soon) to help out with some of the details that we found ourselves doing on the morning of our wedding.

We didn't relax on the wedding morning – we worked, putting the final details of the day together. I'm not saying that this isn't memorable. I look back on it with so much love and respect for our wonderful friends who helped us pull it all together. I wish we could have had a bit more "chill" time before the ceremony though, instead of sprinting to the little summer house where I was whipped into hair and makeup and rushed through the "getting ready" experience with my crew.

Another example of us saving money was collecting all the cutlery and crockery for the wedding day, saving our caterer an extra journey out to the wedding venue which was an hour out of the city. Three weeks out from the wedding I happily agreed to do this task, eager to save some money. We did it, but realized later that our time would have been far better spent socializing with our friends and family who had traveled to celebrate with us, rather than saving $300 on transportation costs. I'm all for being a tight ass, but be mindful when making deals and pick your money-saving battles.

When it comes to wanting to save cash, it doesn't make you cheap for not wanting to spend $50,000 (or more) on your wedding; in fact, I think it makes you smart! Your life together – travel, mortgages, nice dinners, paying bills – will continue after your wedding, and what better way to kick off that phase than to be secure in the knowledge that you didn't go mad with the wedding costs and that you aren't in debt?

I'm going to share lots of ways to be more mindful of your wedding spending. In the wedding business, the notion that you get what you pay for isn't necessarily always true. Many of my podcast guests have suggested that the biggest advantage to save money is lateral thinking: using your network, talking to vendors about who they would recommend (this is such a big and wonderfully great suggestion that is completely underutilized) and stepping away from meaningless traditions to make your own traditions. I often have to remind Bridechillas that a wedding, although a romantic and dreamy day, is also probably the second biggest business transaction in your personal life, behind buying a house (and possibly a car). The most important trick to stick to a wedding budget is – wait for it

– actually having a budget. No shit, Aleisha! It may be obvious, but you would be surprised by how many couples avoid tracking their costs and spending. Having no budget can be the start of some real headaches. It's easy to spend money you don't have until someone wants you to pay that money back.

Creating a wedding budget together and deciding what you are willing to spend on your wedding day is a huge joint decision. Don't deny yourself this exercise as it will strengthen your relationship and, if you have it in writing, help with any heated pre-wedding discussions that may or may not occur. Start your planning process off the right way by communicating and being honest about your expectations for spending and what you each think is reasonable.

AVOID DOUCHEBAGS

Some people in the wedding industry are douchebags and time wasters. They give the whole industry a bad name. They're people who take advantage of couples. They overpromise and under-deliver, overcharge and disappoint. Maybe you've already met some of those people?

I'm sorry.

They are not our people.

They are not Bridechilla vendors. Over the past few years, I have met some of the most generous and kind people who genuinely care about their clients. They will go out of their way to be flexible with the budget and their services where they can. But every industry has people who let the team down; trust me, I worked in television for more than 12 years. If you meet any of the people that I'm talking about, the dodgy vendors that give you bad feelings, then no matter what they are offering, the easiest solution is to walk away and give your business to people that will do a great job with an even better attitude!

MIX IT UP

There are many assumptions in the wedding industry that couples will follow the path of tradition and convention because it is "just what you do." For example, the running order of the wedding day generally follows the plan of arrival, wedding and party. But what if you have a pre-mingle, some drinks and chats with your guests and then hit them with the ceremony? What if you spend the morning of your wedding with your partner and arrive together?

Giving yourself permission to step outside of the conventional way of doing things can be very liberating, especially if certain traditions don't fit in with what you want. There really are no rules and I am certain when you take the first steps to mess with the "norm", you will soon see the possibility of changing other details of your wedding day that perhaps you hadn't questioned or considered before.

I say planning your wedding is a business transaction, but the difference between this transaction and other business transactions is that planning a wedding is emotional. No matter how level-headed you are, it's a day about celebrating your feelings. Some of you may have fantasized about your "dream day" since pre-school! These super-charged emotions and expectations can often blur budget-ary constraints and create a hazy cloud of want, no matter what the cost.

We become attached to "things," thinking these "things" have to be perfect (which doesn't exist), and if these "things" aren't perfect or don't happen, they can lead to meltdowns. I'm all about nurturing Bridechillas and Groomchillas and banishing the Bridezilla shit. It's not where you want to be.

Planning a wedding is not a regular, everyday thing. Organizing a catered event for dozens (hundreds?) of your closest friends and family doesn't come naturally to most people, so I can see how some Bridechillas turn into so-called Bridezillas. Some people get swept up in it all and become temporary A-holes, but that's not going to be you. No way. Not with this book to help you.

BRIDECHILLA BUDGET BASICS

Remember, the easiest way to keep a budget is to keep it simple. Allocate funds for each category of spending. Having a 10% contingency fund for additional expenses will save you from having to make choices on the fly or having to borrow money or sacrifice things that you want to include in your wedding. If you don't spend it, good for you! That's extra money in your pocket. And if you do cheat then you must think of my dad, Dave, saying, "You're only cheating yourself" every time.

BRIDECHILLA STEPS

> **Remember it's a big day, but it's only one day.**
> **Set a budget and stick to it to avoid going into debt.**
> **Don't make big decisions under duress.**
> **Open a wedding bank account and use only that money for the wedding.**
> **Keep track of spending with a notebook or spreadsheet.**
> **NO CHEATING!**

To me, a Bridechilla is a person who realizes that marrying the person you love is way more important than all of the details. So maybe you couldn't find the perfect shade of red for your tablecloths. A Bridechilla is able to keep perspective because she knows it's not about tablecloths. It's about beginning your life with your love.

Bridechilla Lauren

Bridechilla
Side Hustles
Saving and earning money

HAVING A SIDE HUSTLE, working an additional job and using your skills to pay the bills outside of your day job, can be an awesome way to avoid debt and afford the little details that might not be possible on your current budget. I have always been a schemer and a side hustler, looking for ways to make my money work for me so I could get ahead.

When I was 20, I ran a business making jewelry out of bike chains in our garage. I sold to thirty surf stores around the country and won an Australian national business award and a trip to the U.S. to speak at a conference with other young entrepreneurs. It was one of the least complicated businesses out there. I bought bike chains and cleaned the grease off them in a three-step process (involving carcinogenic chemicals, yay!). Then I split the chains, added clasps, and sold them as bracelets and necklaces. I found interesting chains, even gold plated, from all over the place and I expanded the brand by making jewelry out of dominoes and scrabble pieces. Anything I could drill a hole through and chuck around my neck or wrist, hey presto, jewelry!

At the same time, I was studying at university and waitressing. The ROI from this venture didn't make me a bunch of money, but it ignited a passion to run a creative enterprise, and this is a big part of what drives me each day with Bridechilla!

We all have skills and passions that we might not use in our day job, but we could easily monetize. Whether it be teaching or craft, there are plenty of opportunities to market and sell these skills on a part-time or freelance basis. Starting a side hustle is not for everyone. They take time to build, but if you are focused and do your research into what people need and want in your area, it could be a great extra project to add to your wedding planning time line. Recently, Bridechilla

Irene posted in the Bridechilla Community that she had finally paid off her post-wedding credit card bill with help from her side hustle:

> In addition to my day job in web design, I became a freelance dog walker, ramped up my cat-sitting biz/hobby, sold some furniture, and attended some paid focus groups! At an average of about $450/month over our 18-month engagement, it paid for half of the wedding. And yes, I was feeding and medicating cats up until the day of our rehearsal, ha!

FOCUS GROUPS

Supplement your income with your opinion! Market research is happening every day all over the world. Businesses pay market research companies to get people's feedback on their products and brands. Whether that involves reviewing a website from home, tasting a pizza in a lab, or watching a TV show, there are plenty of opportunities to make some extra income by just saying what you think. Visit fgfinder.com to find local groups.

UPWORK OR FIVERR

I often talk about the benefits of using freelancing websites for hiring people to help you with wedding planning tasks, but in this instance perhaps we can flip it around and see what sort of side hustle gigs you could do for someone else.

Maybe you have excellent graphic design skills or are super organized and could spare a couple of hours a day to be someone's virtual assistant by helping them manage their email inbox or respond to Facebook messages. Joining a freelance website like Fiverr or UpWork is quick and easy, and you can start applying for jobs within minutes. Bridechilla Kaycie says:

> I've started babysitting again and became a Beachbody Coach, mainly for the fitness (I've always wanted to lose weight, now seems as good a time as any). I just got my first commission check, and that's exciting. Babysitting - I used to be a full-time nanny and because I adore her and her parents know I'm a poor millennial, they pay me well. I'm using my side hustles as a retirement fund since my current job doesn't offer one. Any spare for wedding goodies will just be a bonus.

IF YOU GENUINELY LOVE SOMETHING, BECOME AN AFFILIATE

Like Bridechilla Kaycie becoming a Beachbody coach (I love the workout programs and have also considered doing this as a side hustle), you can investigate whether a brand or program you have an interest or passion in has an affiliate program. In these kinds of programs you can earn cash for recommending and driving traffic to their website or store. This isn't for everyone, but the industry has changed a lot since Avon and Tupperware parties. Etsy, for example, has an excellent affiliate program that pays 8% for sales via your recommended links. I use it all the time. I genuinely enjoy finding awesome Etsy products to share with the community, so it matches my interests, and I know that it will work for our audience. Investigate some of your favorite brands. You'd be surprised as to how many have referral bonuses and programs. Bridechilla Nicole Marie says:

> I started selling Mary Kay for our wedding in February 2018. I'm not the greatest sales person, so I haven't made much, but my skin is now flawless.

RENTING YOUR STUFF/HOUSE

If you travel a lot for work, or if you have a spare room and feel like it might be a good space to rent out, consider listing it on Airbnb. I recently worked with a gal who was funding her kitchen renovations by renting their spare room for three nights per week. She was rather wily by undercutting their closest competitor by a couple of dollars and providing bread and spreads and tea and coffee for breakfast (something other listings weren't doing). This option isn't for everyone, but if you live in a commuter area, big city, or somewhere near an airport, this can be an easy income earner. Bridechilla Amber has combined a few side hustles:

> Dog walking, babysitting, Airbnbing my second bedroom!

The benefits of side hustles for many Bridechillas can outweigh the disadvantages, but be mindful that overnight success with side hustles are rare and they do require time. Consider the return on your time investment and the cost of set up (website, craft items, software) before jumping in and making the commitment. I've heard marvelous stories of side hustles turning into full-time jobs, especially in creative industries; however, if you are already stressed and overworked, think carefully before taking the plunge.

BRIDECHILLA STEPS

> **Side hustles are great if you have the time to make it work.**
> **Don't take on new stress and pressure if it isn't conducive to your budget and mental health.**
> **Commit to one great side hustle, don't try and take on a million tasks.**

A Bridechilla is someone who decides what's important to her and ditches the rest. The things a Bridechilla worries about are decisions made consciously – not because the industry tells us it's important or a family member thinks it's important.

Bridechilla Jessica

Wedding Donors

**How to avoid
"I'll pay, but do it my way"**

PLANNING A WEDDING IS A BIT like participating in an election. Some people self-fund their campaigns and go it alone, while others have well-endowed donors who generously contribute to their cause.

Like political campaigns, donors often present themselves under the guise of just wanting to support their candidate. They believe in them and want them to have the best opportunity to achieve their goals! They may claim that there are no strings attached to their donations, that decisions should be made in the best interests of the candidate and to promote their ethos and choices along the way. We know this to be a big bag of bullshit as one of the most lucrative jobs in politics is the lobbyist, someone who works on behalf of industry and donors. Lobbyists bargain and negotiate. They schmooze, and if you've seen *House Of Cards*, you'll know that some are very persuasive and attractive and are worth leaving politics for. Remy Danton, I am looking at you.

Accepting money for your wedding is akin to accepting political donations. There will be people who generously offer money with no requests, guilt, or qua-si-blackmail. There will be a lot of people who offer money but then want something in return – to control the guest list, to come to every appointment, to be copied on every wedding-planning email.

This is not to say that these are conscious, well-thought-out manipulations triggered by some grand master plan to completely control your wedding; but more often than not the generous contributions by parents or family members can quickly go from "let us help you" to a political minefield.

CONDITIONAL GENEROSITY = FAUX GENEROSITY

I call this conditional generosity, whereby wedding donors generously offer you cash to help pay for your wedding, but it comes with strings attached. This fine print can be anything from inviting a bunch of friends that you've never met, demanding you get married in a church even though you are atheists, or your mother insisting on shitty chair covers because she thinks the chairs look "tacky". All of these are real-life examples from Bridechillas.

Perhaps you have experienced conditional generosity in other parts of your life. Someone is nice to you, but you realize there is a catch, or that their niceness also brings them something. Perhaps you've been emotionally blackmailed: when you've done something because you think that if you don't your friendship would suffer, or the other person will ditch you as a friend. I know I have, and most of the time I didn't figure out what was happening until much later.

If some of your wedding donors are pulling these moves, there are solutions and ways to salvage the situation without big fights or any drama. I want to reiterate that I am positive most wedding donors don't do this on purpose, but pulling these moves can cause more trouble and stress than not having donors at all.

As we've learned, your money story originates with your parents. Their dealings with money are the foundation of how we work our finances, and in some cases, if they are bad with cash, the kids have been inspired to flip it and reverse it and get their shit together.

Before we jump into some solutions to conditional generosity and decreasing any over-involvement or pushiness when it comes to, "I'm paying for this so you should do it my way," let's remember a few subtle but important things about parents, even if they are cool:

- In the good old days, the 1970s and 1980s, it was still pretty common for parents to be hands-on with their kid's wedding and fund it.
- When our parents got married (if they did), your grandparents probably paid for it and "managed a lot of details," including inviting a bunch of their friends.
- Pinterest, donut walls, dudes as bridesmaids and ditching some of the formality are probably new concepts to them and challenge the way that they see weddings as a whole.

I was at a big, somewhat-awful wedding fair in London last year, roaming around with my microphone interviewing people for the podcast and I found that the most receptive people to speak with were the moms and mother-in-laws. Most of them were either completely overwhelmed, their heads turning like fair clowns, or they were digging it, with their arms full of shopping bags and brochures. I asked them what had changed since they got hitched and what they hoped for their child's wedding.

Most of the responses focused on how much of a hullabaloo weddings have become. How complicated the event has become and how much time and money goes into organizing it. They recollected that when they got married, they just booked a church and a hall, got married, had a three-hour dinner and dance and then went on their honeymoon – finito. There were two extremes in their thought processes:

- They LOVED all the fuss and extra stuff and felt deep regret that they didn't get to have that at their wedding (warning signs here).
- They think it's all a bit ridiculous and question why the hell you need a DJ and a band and perish the thought that you might have a non-traditional reading in the ceremony. Cue the alarm bells!

The moms that felt they missed out wanted to be more involved (which can be nice but also intense). The other moms who felt that it was all over the top were also involved, but more from the point of view of challenging newer aspects of weddings. They were fraught with worry that their kids were going rogue and that they would look like idiots among their friends.

Whatever camp your parents fit into – and maybe they're totally cool – like all Bridechilla approaches to problem-solving, this one comes down to communication. So much of the time we argue and get confused because of misinformation and misunderstanding different perspectives. Parents can feel like they are out of the loop and freak out when they don't know things. They often assume that their kids are going to plan their wedding the way they planned theirs. Without access to information, they jump to these conclusions. So, if you don't tell, they don't know.

When it comes to contributing funds to your wedding, it's important to have a conversation about their expectations of that money. If you have this conversation, and yes I know talking about money can be uncomfortable, you will all know where you stand.

- Is their contribution to be added to the overall budget?
- Do they have specific expectations for their contributions?
- Do they want you to pay for specific things with this money – caterer? Wedding dress?
- Do they want to see receipts and spreadsheets?

- How involved are they hoping to be?
- Does this money come with conditions? Guest list additions?

I'm certainly not saying that you need to keep them abreast of all moves, decisions, and processes; however, making small changes to your communication style from the get-go can solve a lot of issues. If everyone knows how the money is going to be used, and you are open about it, it is a lot less likely to get confusing further down the track.

One mother at a wedding fair confided in me (and my microphone!) that she felt a bit like a bank, as if she were a wedding ATM, and she only attended the wedding show to see where all of her money was going. I felt a little bit sorry for everyone involved in her story because from her perspective she felt taken advantage of, but I could see her daughter's point of view that she was planning her wedding and her mom happened to offer the money.

I didn't get the impression that the mom was a control freak or wanted to boss her daughter around, she just wanted to feel like she was a part of it and that her contributions were being used "wisely." I put "wisely" in quotation marks because inevitably we all have a difference of opinion regarding how money should be spent and what we find valuable. This is even more apparent when we add generational differences to the mix.

For many of us, we aren't always going to agree with our parents or other donors on how money should be spent. Some people are reactionary and say things that are hurtful, or try and use their generosity to their advantage to get their own way. A typical emotional blackmail tactic is to make you feel bad or obliged to do something because the other person has been so gracious to help you out (conditional generosity).

Often calmly pointing out that you are stressed and that their actions might be causing you to feel overwhelmed and pressured can help them see your point of view and ease the situation. I guarantee if you lay it all out there, sit down with a cup of tea or vodka and have an open conversation about your expectations and the donor's expectations, that you will all feel more informed and open to each other's perspectives. Set boundaries. Understand who is paying for what. Are there limits? Are there strings?

If this isn't something that you think you can do, or your parents or wedding donors aren't into compromises or hearing your perspective, the simple solution is to not take the cash. Avoid the issues altogether.

Have the wedding you want without the obligation and pressure of having to answer to other people. Sure, their money might be helpful and give you more freedom to do what you want, but to what end? Be bold. Open up and own it.

STEPFAMILIES AND EXTENDED FAMILIES

Families come in different shapes and sizes and none are perfect because, as we know, perfection doesn't exist. Divorce, separation, feuds and disputes affect families and friendships every day. Since weddings are generally family focused events, it can be hard to avoid being sucked into the vortex of he said/she said and ridiculous shit that people can pull when they're potentially angry, confused and bitter. Something you may face if you are dealing with a challenging stepfamily and extended family situation is trying to divert attention away from the past and help family members focus on the love and celebration of your wedding. My hope is that families can put aside their differences and act like mature, sensible adults, and understand that bringing their emotional baggage into your wedding planning is inappropriate and selfish.

Unfortunately, behavioral blinders are worn by many people, especially in the matters of the heart. Managing these situations can be easier said than done and, for many of us, juggling the expectations of others can be difficult and even upsetting.

I've had a number of listeners contact me with scenarios that involve ultimatums and threats of parents not attending or taking back money that they'd promised to give because their ex is attending or some other bullshit excuse. All of these situations can be avoided if parents and extended parties temporarily put aside their differences and issues, and tolerate and respect the child/family member's special day.

It can be very hard to give advice in these situations, but I can say confidently that it helps to keep calm and focus on creating a happy and peaceful day. Try not to take these actions personally. Communicating with family about how their behavior is affecting you in a negative way can also go a long way to rectifying the situation. Or at least they might try to remember that their behavior is not worthy of distracting and upsetting you.

POSITIVE BLENDED FAMILY INCLUSIONS

There are many ways to celebrate and be inclusive of blended and stepfamilies in your wedding. Perhaps you or your partner has been married before or your parents have remarried and you are looking for ways to include your extended family in your wedding celebrations.

Being gracious and inclusive goes a long way. Often people just want to feel involved and know that their opinion matters to you. If you have had stepparents and stepsiblings in your life for a long time (and you like them), it might be nice to find a special moment to share with them on your wedding day like a dance, or a speech. Their involvement doesn't have to shadow your parents' role in your wedding – it should be seen more as a complimentary inclusion.

If either you or your partner have children from a previous relationship, you can include them in your wedding service in a few different ways. Perhaps you can walk down the aisle with your children or, if they're old enough, you can ask them to help with a wedding reading. You can also add a special line or two into the ceremony about the importance of raising children with love and happiness together.

BRIDECHILLA STEPS

> **Plan a family meeting to talk about your budget. Be clear and concise about your expectations and theirs.**
> **If you disagree with your wedding donor's opinions or wants, try and find a middle ground. Communication and honesty will always be your friend.**

today is the tomorrow you
worried about yesterday

Being a Bridechilla is about having the emotional intelligence to allow yourself some freak outs, yet still be able to get over it and move on with the day/ month/year if things don't all go perfectly as planned.

Bridechilla Ezela

Opinions
How to deflect them
like Wonder Woman

FOR MANY COUPLES, marriage is as much about creating new family relationships as it is creating their own partnership. Entering into any close family relationship, especially combining that experience with the sometimes-stressful situation of planning a wedding, can be full on. FULL ON. Also, families can be weird. Fact.

Often it takes a new person joining the fold to make you realize just how weird families can be. Eccentricities and habits mixed with expectations and their "own way of doing things" can lead to behavior that isn't exactly first class. I guarantee you that opinions are the gift that keeps on giving throughout your engagement. As the very wise saying goes, "Opinions are like assholes; everyone's got one."

Everyone has something to say and no matter how helpful they think they are being, it can be damn frustrating, especially when dealing with money. The opinion givers believe that by telling you just how much their idea is worth considering, even when you are confident with your choices, you will suddenly change your plans or realize what a genius they are. When wedding donors are involved, opinions can be pretty hard to ignore or deflect.

Sometimes people's opinions are offered because they truly believe they know better than you. Other times it comes back to the fear of ignoring traditions. If you are going off the book with your plans, and someone is worried about how it will affect them, it's important to remember that some people react in silly ways when their own way of thinking is challenged.

So how do you deal with unwanted opinions and nosiness without being a jerk? One of my favorite opinion-slaying sayings comes from Oprah, OF COURSE! I love it because it demonstrates how relatable and bloody great that lady is. The simplicity and power of the phrase has a tinge of finality about it, yet isn't too rude. You ready?

"That's not going to work for me."

What I love about this saying is that it is direct, but polite. The opinion giver doesn't have much opportunity to reply. If you want to soften the blow, you can add, "Thanks so much for thinking of me/us. That's a good idea, but it's not going to work for us." That way their opinion has been heard, but they aren't under the impression that you are going to change your plans or follow their course of action just because they suggested it. Avoiding offense can be a delicate and complicated process and it is hard to be strong enough to use your voice. Working as a team with your partner – to create the wedding that you want while avoiding being strong-armed into doing what others would like you to do – isn't always easy. It requires resilience and commitment to the cause, but trust me when I say it will be worth it.

Of course, the cliché of the overbearing mother-in-law is often just that, a cliché. But in any situation, you are entering into a new family which may have different ways of doing things and different ideas about what a wedding should be. Be empowered to make choices and stick with them.

Being a Bridechilla is about being chilled out and relaxed and not getting stressed, but it's also about being empowered. It's about finding your voice and confidence to make choices that are good for you as a couple and to communicate that with family and friends and vendors without being rude or an asshole.

I find it interesting when opinions of parents and in-laws are driven by worry that they will be "judged" for your decisions, instead of worry for the decision itself. We worry what people will think of our Facebook photos, and our parents worry about what your third cousin Cheryl will think of you wearing a colored wedding dress.

Often when it's your own parents, it can be easier just to say, "Please stop. Please shut up. Please, for the love of God shut up."

However, when it is your mother-in-law or your partner's auntie, it may not be as easy or appropriate to tell them to shut their traps. Deep breathing exercises are excellent, as is wine. Here are some steps to keep it all calm and hopefully to nurture your relationship with your in-laws and new family.

BLOCK IT OUT

OK, this isn't the most mature piece of advice to kick it all off but bear with me. I'm hoping if you are planning a wedding, you have chosen to marry your partner because you like them – hopefully a lot! You laugh at the same stuff, you're comfortable sitting around in stretchy pants without wearing a bra, you acknowledge that you lie to each other about how often you floss your teeth. These are all aspects of your relationship that make you the most fabulous couple ever. You get each other. You aren't marrying your MIL. This isn't her wedding and no matter how much she might try to make it about her – ahem, it ain't. Your wedding day is about celebrating the oddities and the love and the commitment that you share with your significant other. A big part of these oddities, and probably where they came from in the first place, is family. When in-laws are difficult, I recommend taking the path of suffocating the situation (not the person) with love (or wine) and understanding, as Cher would say. If all else fails, move on to the next step.

PATIENCE

Uniting two families can be a case of two worlds colliding. You're bringing people together that probably wouldn't be friends or know each other in everyday life. Each family has different ways of doing things, different histories, different traditions, different belief systems, different sporting teams and certainly different expectations of their child's wedding day. So whenever you are confronted with an odd statement such as, "That's not what I'd do," or, "In our family, we only eat yellow things," take a moment, breathe, and ask, why are they acting this way?

The simple answer could just be that your MIL is an A-hole who deep down believes that you are stealing her child, "Who should have married Brittany when they had the chance." But guess what MIL? They didn't pick Brittany so move on already. Move on.

Alternatively, if you peel back the layers of advice and bossiness, I'm betting MIL just really wants to be a part of planning your wedding and doesn't really know how to communicate that without making you want to take an extra Ambien or three.

GET THEM INVOLVED

Now I'm sure a few of you are reading this thinking "Lady, the problem is that my MIL is already far too involved and I need her to back off! This is terrible advice." But stick with me. We're going to use a little bit of reverse psychology to massage the situation. The trick is to help your MIL *feel* like she's making decisions, when you are really just allocating her jobs and organizational tasks that will allow her to be involved (and appreciated) without taking over.

Perhaps invite your MIL to taste the cake or, if you really like her, to share a special moment like the dress fitting. If she's really keen to "be more hands-on," get her to fold every one of those goddamned DIY, origami, pop-up save the date cards that you bought on Etsy and thought would be easy but actually requires an engineering PhD. Maybe MIL is a whizz-bang cook and would love to cater your engagement party or host your bridal shower for you?

COMMUNICATION AND WORKING TOGETHER

A lot of the time issues occur because people don't realize how they are behaving; sometimes you've just got tell them. I'm not talking about being rude, I'm talking about being assertive. If your future in-laws are being overly opinionated and you are struggling to see their view, you can let them know in the clearest and most level-headed way possible that you appreciate their input but you will be taking a different path. "I like your second cousin Darleen, but I don't know her well enough for her to be a bridesmaid in our wedding. Your advice is really valuable and it means a lot to me, but the bridal party is already locked in." Or perhaps even, "We've had some time to think about having our wedding in your garage, but as we've already paid the deposit on the vineyard, we think we'll stick to the plan. Thanks for the generous offer!"

If the polite approaches aren't working, then revert to our favorite assertive phrase, "That's not going to work for me." If that doesn't do the trick, then smile, hold eye contact, and edge backward. When you are far enough away, turn around and run.

EXPECTATIONS

Managing expectations, both your own and those of your family and friends, is one of the most challenging aspects of being a Bridechilla. We spend a lot of time thinking about how we want things to look, hoping people will act a certain way, worrying if it will all come together, and second-guessing if people will have a good time at your wedding celebrations. These are all expectations. A lot of the time when expectations aren't met, or the outcome is different from how you expected it to be, it can really throw you off track.

Parents and older folk might have expectations that you are going to organize a traditional wedding. Often they will encourage you to "do what you want, it's your wedding," but when it comes down to it and you choose to take a different direction, all of a sudden their expectations are not being met and trouble brews. They can't deal with it.

It's okay to be disappointed when things don't go to plan. It's totally normal. We attach a lot of emotion to wedding planning because, even before we get engaged, there is pressure and expectations placed upon us for things to be successful and "go right."

All we can do is our best. If things aren't going to plan and you feel overwhelmed by the expectations, then take a step back, be calm, and find a solution.

If other people's expectations and pressure are bothering you, then either take a step back and disconnect from them for a moment or let them know that the way they are communicating is not helping you achieve what you want and move forward.

For example, if your mom thinks you should be a long-haired, thin bride when in fact you are a curvy short-haired bride, then her expectations are unrealistic. You have to shut that shit down. It's not always easy, but maintaining focus and control and keeping your Chilla perspective will help you succeed.

BE STRONG MY FRIEND

Remember, keeping the peace doesn't have to equal being a pushover. Set your boundaries early. This is your opportunity to get everything square because (hopefully) you'll be hanging around with your MIL and new extended family for a long time. If your MIL can see that you are a strong person, someone who won't be maligned, who loves their child and is in a team with them, then that is the best you can do.

It may not always be easy or smooth, but by working together to build the foundations of a strong relationship and figuring out all of the family shit that can come along, it's only going to make things easier for all of you down the track. This is especially true during challenging times, which are inevitable for all of us in some way or another.

Remember Bridechillas try and see things from other people's perspectives, even if it's challenging for them. The issues that you may be experiencing with your in-laws may be symptoms of other problems that are happening in their lives. Perhaps they aren't listening to *The Bridechilla Podcast* and have yet to see the value in open pathways of communication. Instead they may channel their opinions and needs into passive-aggressive statements or idle threats. We know that's not the path to succeeding, but by trying to see their point of view, you can position yourself to swoop in and force their hand with better communication.

Be mindful, be caring and be strong. Get your partner on board and rock the hell out of it.

BRIDECHILLA STEPS

> **Commit to clear communication and patience. Be the bigger person.**
> **If people are being overly opinionated, take a breath and consider your reaction before going for it. Understand that some families don't communicate well and might need a bit of gentle guidance.**

For me, being a Bridechilla is about being authentic, and making your wedding a reflection of your relationship and life together. It's remembering that how things FEEL is more important than how things LOOK.

Bridechilla Lauren

It's OK to Feel Like Shit

I CONSIDER MYSELF to be a relatively optimistic and upbeat member of society, but like any other human, sometimes I feel sad or overwhelmed with responsibility and pressure and I feel like crawling into bed and watching three seasons of *The Real Housewives of Orange County* while eating an entire jar of Nutella. Just because you're engaged to someone you really like (let's upgrade that to LOVE), you're planning a wedding and creating lots of wonderful memories together, doesn't mean you have to be happy all the time.

Pick up a wedding magazine or watch a pop-up advertisement from a big name jeweler or wedding gown company and you will notice a pattern. Everyone's losing their shit with happiness. There's an energy that surrounds the wedding media and advertising – I get it, they want to sell us stuff – but the message is that every couple is 100% happy during every stage of the process. We are told we must enjoy every single moment, that we will all get along, and everything will go to plan.

Unless you are a billionaire and on crack, this is a total fallacy. And realistically even billionaires have family issues, probably more so than most because they've got all that coin. The perception of ultimate 100% happiness and perfection is not real, and once we realize this, we allow ourselves to embrace the moment as it is. I received an email from a Bridechilla Graduate, Sara, who summed this up in such a way that had me laughing, nodding and high-fiving strangers:

> We had a first look and family photos before the ceremony. During the family photos, my wedding planner casually came up and said, "Don't freak out, but there's an RV on fire on top of the mountain pass, and the caterer, DJ and two-thirds of your guests are stuck behind it. The highway patrol is saying two hours until it's cleared." My first thought was no big deal, we have plenty of booze. We delayed the ceremony an hour, and instead of sitting in hiding I mingled with my guests, had cocktails, and great conversations. I've never been

so happy for a fire to delay anything. Without your advice, I'd never have been so chill. Aleisha, I can't thank you enough for what you do. I'm a high-strung valium-popping lady, and I swear I didn't have anxiety once on my wedding day. My cheeks hurt from smiling and my feet hurt from dancing. Thank you for chilling me out and helping me to know to fuck chair covers.

Bridechilla Sara and her partner embraced the chaos, and in the end, it made their day even more memorable. If Sara can do it, so can you. Perfection doesn't exit.*

DITCHING THE QUEST FOR PERFECTION

As we know, perfection doesn't exist. Risk-taking and wedding planning are not often connected, but I think one of the keys to being a Bridechilla is taking risks, trusting your gut, and doing shit that lots of other brides just wouldn't do.

Being prepared for things that might go wrong is sensible, but don't allow yourself to be overcome by what ifs. If Sara hadn't embraced that RV fire and pivoted to the mindset of using the time to mingle with her guests, she would have been waiting it out nervously, probably over-thinking what else could go wrong, instead of having an amazing time at her own wedding.

Going through the wedding planning process knowing that some people will not understand your decisions, and that some vendors might not be the right fit for you, is a great start. If you feel confident that you can cope with whatever comes your way and work as a team to solve any hiccups, then you are going to be just fine.

We invest a lot of time and energy and money into planning our wedding. As I've said throughout this book, your wedding day is just the beginning of the adventure. It's one day or a weekend in a long and wonderful journey. I'm not an advocate of wishing your life away, but I assure you that in six or twelve months' time, when your wedding is but a memory, you will look back on stressful moments, decisions, and opportunities with positivity.

I'm not going to pretty this up, there will be challenges, and you will be forced to realize that not everything will be as easy as the wedding magazines say. People will behave weirdly. You'll have to make choices about who to invite, who is important to you and how much money to spend. Surrounding yourself with people who understand you and making sure that your decisions are supported by your partner are amazing foundations for your life together.

Yes, shit will go down. You'll have highs and lows when it comes to decisions surrounding your wedding, but if you can get through this, you can get through anything. Some days you will want nothing to do with wedding planning, and that is absolutely fine. Listen to your body, listen to your mind, and make sure you step away from the computer and give yourself time to breathe and be normal.

Here is the truth: Sometimes you are not going to feel like looking at vendor quotes or spending time on Pinterest or doing any sort of wedding planning at all and that is A-OK.

Wedding planning slumps are completely legit and I liken it to training for a marathon. You have to pace yourself. You're not running 26 miles every day – if you are, you're a freak athlete and I respect you deeply. Take a break, have a wine and feel smug with your superhuman achievements.

Sometimes we can get so wrapped up in this process that we forget about the outside world. Make sure you schedule real-life time where you watch the TV and go out and speak to friends about all the things that are happening in their life that aren't associated with seating plans and table runners.

Date nights are crucial. It's easy to get into a wedding planning funk where you spend all your waking hours just talking about this one day. Being present and involved in life outside of wedding planning can be challenging, but it is also vital for maintaining sanity and your chill.

If you enter a wedding planning slump, embrace it! Go and do something else and come back to the folders and the spreadsheets when you get the urge. Nothing is too important that it can't be done on the weekend or next week. If I'm feeling creatively uninspired, I need to walk away from the project, go for a run, have a drink with friends, listen to music, go to the movies, do something else that isn't the task at hand and figure out why I'm not feeling motivated. Then I return re-energized with a new path and solution to my creative block.

If you are truly feeling unmotivated and lackluster about wedding planning and you haven't considered hiring a wedding planner or coordinator to work with, then this may be the beacon that you need to explore that option.

In the Bridechilla Community Facebook group, there was a discussion about stress and health. Some of the Bridechillas were talking about dealing with IBS, colitis and Crohn's disease. They spoke about the possibility of a flare-up of their condition during wedding planning or their wedding celebrations and shared ways that they were hoping to maintain their health during this period.

What struck me about the group was the honesty and openness about a pretty personal topic. I was proud that community members were keen to share and support each other because, especially in the world of weddings, it can be hard to say, "Actually, I'm not having a great time because I feel like shit and my health is suffering." There is an onus on women to put on a brave face and be stoic. For some unknown reason we must simply enjoy every single moment of wedding planning (and life), and if not, we are considered ungrateful. It's very strange, patriarchal bullshit. Physical and mental health issues cannot simply be switched off or forgotten about because you are planning a wedding. The perception that everything should be amazing all the time is nonsense and unrealistic.

I challenge Bridechillas to be open and discuss the issues that affect their lives. We should be able to speak about anxiety, depression and mental illness in the same manner as we discuss physical health problems. When it comes to mental health, so many of us will be affected either personally or via a loved one. It is completely normal. The sooner we learn to accept and speak freely about mental health issues, the more people will be empowered to learn about how to support each other during tough periods. Experiencing health problems should not be something that you feel shame about in any way.

When we discuss mental health issues in the Bridechilla Community, many members express relief and feel reassured that they are not alone in going through this. Anxiety and depression can be debilitating. You can feel helpless and hopeless. Pessimism can override thoughts of happiness and happy endings. Simple tasks can be overwhelming; planning for the future, let alone focusing on choosing details for a wedding, can feel like a burden.

When someone who doesn't understand depression or anxiety says, "Just cheer up," or, "Smile, it will make you feel better," it can make you want to punch them, or scream. Surrounding yourself with people who "get" you, understand you and can give you space if you need it is the most important thing to do until you are better and ready to roll. This overrides every other wedding planning decision. Your good health and mental stability, being able to look after yourself and your loved ones, is very important. If wedding planning is affecting your health in a negative way, then it's time to step back, press pause and focus on what is most important to you.

If people are challenged by your health condition and you feel comfortable in communicating how you feel and how it affects you, then I challenge you to talk about it. It's a small but bold step, choosing to be truly honest about your condition (or your partner's condition) that will instigate positive change in the perception of health and wellness.

Although wedding planning can feel like a full-time job, it doesn't have to be that way. If you feel overwhelmed, seek help. If you need time off, take it. Don't be afraid to ask for help and delegate tasks that don't work with your schedule.

Your time is precious and the sooner your value your time, the sooner you can take control and make wedding planning decisions that work positively for you. As in any situation, there will always be someone on social media who looks like they have a freaking fantastic time every second of the day. No doubt you have a friend who is constantly posting about how easy wedding planning is, or how on-budget they are, or what a perfect day their wedding is going to be. But I will bet you one million Bridechilla dollars** that she is putting on a very convenient façade like so many people do in the age of social media. Her wedding planning is probably a shit show. It can be challenging to block out these external factors, to not compare your budget and the look of your wedding to something you've seen on Pinterest. But you need to maintain focus on what your wedding is really about: you and your fellow weirdo standing in front of your closest family and friends and making a commitment to put up with each other's weird shit, create millions of in-jokes, support each other through the good times and not so good times, and hopefully stay together and enjoy each other's company for many years to come.

BRIDECHILLA STEPS

> **Life is complicated. Unexpected shit comes along all the time. If you feel overwhelmed or stressed, cut yourself some slack. Breathe. Have a vodka or a cup of tea and breathe some more.**
> **Take time away from planning and logistics and live, damn it, LIVE!**
> **Know that perfection and the push for planning the "best day" isn't healthy, nor is it enjoyable.**
> **Know that this is just the beginning of your adventure together. Work as a team and laugh at the silliness of it all!**

* Damn you, typos
** Bridechilla dollars have no actual value and are not redeemable for real dollars or bitcoin

A Bridechilla in three(ish) words:
mindfulness, grace,
big-picture-oriented.

Bridechilla Katie

Traditions

Go your own way!

HERE'S SOMETHING THAT you might have already observed during your wedding planning. Parents and older people are obsessed with sticking to tradition, even if the traditions have no meaning or relevance to their lives or your wedding. "Your father isn't exchanging you for one of Tom's family's cows? But it's tradition! You've got to!"

There are many wedding traditions that are completely useless when it comes to modern weddings, and for a lot of couples using these traditions in their weddings is just something they embrace without thinking about, without considering why the tradition existed in the first place. For our parents and older generations, sticking to these traditions is just what you did. Bridechillas and Groomchillas, on the other hand, like to question why they're doing certain things and ditch them if they don't provide any meaning to them personally. Just as it takes people to start traditions, it takes people to end them and create new ones!

You are those people. You are tradition trailblazers, pioneers of new, non-hokey wedding customs, many of which will be shared on Buzzfeed and replicated by millions (that's how society works now, there are no new ideas, just new Buzzfeed ideas). You, my Bridechilla friends, have the power to forge new folklore and banish the banal. No pressure. Bridechillas, you are in the delightful position of ditching some of the more conventional wedding traditions and reinventing others to suit you. There are zero rules. Nada.

Historically, the world of weddings is choc-a-block with old-timey superstitions from yesteryear. When we delve deeper into their beginnings, it's puzzling to see why we have clung on to them for so long, like asking the father's permission for his daughter's hand in marriage and the accompanied parental aisle walk.

Seriously, as nice as it is to have your dad guide you from one end of a room to the other, the origins of those traditions, the transferring of "ownership" of a woman from man to man is, I think, a little on the nose now.

Of course, very few people actually believe they are exchanging their possession, their daughter, as a method of climbing the social hierarchy or increasing land ownership, but I find the idea that so many couples somewhat blindly add this little exchange to their marriage ceremony intriguing.

I am not against traditions; they can be safe and cozy, like popping on your stretchy pants and watching Netflix on a Friday night instead of going out. But sometimes it's nice to shake things up a bit, leave your TV lover at home, and converse with a real person. So, let's expand your options and take a look at a couple of the more traditional aspects of a wedding that you can choose to use, abuse or add your own twist to.

THE MIXED-GENDERED BRIDAL PARTY

Are you keen on having a bridal crew, but you have some guy besties? Include them! Originally the bridesmaid's primary task was to act as a human shield to ward off evil spirits. Dressed identically, bridesmaids were tasked with preventing a hexing by confusing moronic ghouls who didn't know which one the bride was.

In modern times, the bridal party has evolved from sorcery blockers to people who know all your darkest secrets (and then some) and are willing to use their precious holiday leave for your six-day pre-wedding extravaganza. You can have guys-maids, guys-men, bridesmen, groomsmen, grandmas (as I saw one Bridechilla recently choose). Perhaps you want to combine your friends and create an uber bridal party? A mutual A-team?

Removing traditional gender constraints from the bridal party makes it all a lot more fun and it means that you can have whoever you like standing alongside you witnessing your declaration of love. As long as they love and support you, it shouldn't matter what gender, age, or shoe size these folks are.

NOT SEEING EACH OTHER BEFORE THE WEDDING

This old chestnut comes from the times of arranged marriages where it was feared that if the groom met the bride before the wedding and didn't think she was much chop, he'd call off the wedding. Therefore, it became a tradition that the bride and groom were only allowed to meet at the wedding ceremony so that the groom didn't bail.

I am guessing you have met your partner. This is probably not something you need to be concerned with, so if you want to hang out before the wedding and even turn up and walk down the aisle together, go for it. First look photographs, where the couple meets before the ceremony for some photos and quiet moments together, are increasingly the norm. They are great for time-saving (with photography) and also for having a bit of downtime together before the day kicks in. Your wedding day is going to be a fun, exciting day, so why would you want to spend even a bit of it apart?

THE GARTER TOSS

Puke. Sorry. I don't know if it's seeing a guy put his head up a lady's skirt, or the fact that this tradition comes from medieval times where the garter (and ripping other bits off the bride's dress for good luck) was seen as proof of consummation of the marriage. I don't know, there's just something manky about it all. Do as you will, but personally, I skipped this one!

THROWING THE BOUQUET

Again, I have no issue with this tradition, I did it at our wedding and I've enjoyed jumping around like a loon at other people's weddings trying to tackle friends to catch the bouquet. But I have also been one of the few single women at a wedding corralled onto the dance floor to catch flowers like some lonely performing monkey. It wasn't amazing, especially when I attended a friend's wedding a few weeks after canceling my own (the first one that is!).

YOU HAVE TO WEAR WHITE

Nope. You can wear whatever color you like. End of story. Author W. Somerset Maugham said, "Tradition is a guide and not a jailer." If you want the big wedding, the whole shebang, full of customs and traditions, do it! The freedom to marry gives you the freedom to do whatever the hell you want, but do us a favor and make some new traditions that generations to come will be proud to replicate.

VOWS

"To honor and obey" and "until death do us part" – yawn. The ceremony is where you recite your vows and proclaim your commitment to each other. As well as saying all the lovey-dovey stuff, it's where you agree to accept each other's weirdness, to overlook odd hygiene rituals and wardrobe hogging, to make the commitment of marriage and to unite Netflix accounts (otherwise known as wedflix). Forget the decor and music list, the ceremony is the wedding sweet spot. Truly a time where you can let your "couple personality" shine. Add readings that are meaningful to you; ditch the stuffiness and invite friends and family members to contribute. Use a quote from a favorite movie, like *When Harry Met Sally*:

> When you realize you want to spend the rest of your life with somebody, you want the rest of your life to start as soon as possible.

Or something smart for the literati (this whole reading from Plato's *The Symposium* is wonderful):

> And so, when a person meets the half that is his very own...then something wonderful happens: the two are struck from their senses by love, by a sense of belonging to one another, and by desire, and they don't want to be separated from one another, not even for a moment.

Or funny and silly, like all of us, from comedian Rita Rudner:

> I love being married. It's so great to find that one special person you want to annoy for the rest of your life.

NAME CHANGING: TO CHANGE OR NOT TO CHANGE?

The conversation about post-wedding name changes often crops up in the Bridechilla Community and it is a topic that invokes passionate responses, all of which have merit.

I can say comfortably that 99% of Bridechillas would consider themselves feminists. Bridechillas believe in equality for all, and they challenge traditions that aren't meaningful to them or have no purpose in their lives. For some Bridechillas, changing their name is a given and isn't something that they wouldn't consider doing; for others, this is a decision that weighs heavily and it can be difficult to come to the "right" conclusion. Whether you decide to take your partner's name, hyphenate, or make up a whole new one, it is your decision to make and yours alone.

Some believe that there is an expectation that women will automatically decide to change their name because it is "traditional" or "the right thing to do," but for me, it is a decision that shouldn't be made due to feelings of obligation.

Take time to consider what feels right for you. Speak with your partner, be honest about your feelings either way and don't feel pressured to make a decision that you aren't comfortable with. If you choose not to change your name, talk about what name any of your future children will take.

When it came to changing my name, my husband Rich supported me in whatever I wanted. I had a lot of attachment to my surname, McCormack, and I didn't want to let it go entirely. But I also wanted to be a Maddock, my married name, so I concluded that I would compromise (for me, not anyone else) and that I would use McCormack for all of my work (performing and podcasts) and Maddock for "home things". I legally changed my name, and McCormack is my business name. That works very well for me! Whatever you choose, do take the time to think about what works for you. Be sure to throw any opinions of others straight in the fuck it bucket (see next chapter!) because your name is a big part of *your* identity and no one other than you should have a deciding factor over that!

> **Don't just do something because it is tradition, especially if it doesn't suit your tastes.**
> **If you would like to include a tradition but it doesn't match your ethos or style, change it up.**
> **Don't feel pressured by older generations to follow traditions just because it makes them happy.**
> **Get creative! Use the details of traditions you like and ditch the rest!**

A Bridechilla is diplomatic; she speaks up and communicates well.
Not only is she empowered during planning through the community she loves, she's empowered in all aspects of life by knowing it's healthy to be true to one's self.

Bridechilla Anja

The Fuck It Bucket

HERE'S THE DEAL: To get married, you really only need three things. You, your partner, and someone to marry you. That's it. All of the other stuff is fun (and sometimes unnecessary) icing on the cake.

In Bridechilla-land, there are no "have tos" or "musts" – in fact, the Bridechilla ethos is about simplifying the process and removing all the extra tasks, stress, and stuff that we've been told over and over again we need when in reality, they are entirely optional. I've placed this chapter early in the book to enlighten and inspire you to ditch the stress over silly things – stuff you don't really need but feel pressured to include because Pinterest or The Knot says so. You may be including some of the details and tasks found in this chapter in your wedding, and that's great, but if you find yourself worrying about money and time to make these elements happen, then I suggest you throw them straight in the fuck it bucket.

The concept of the fuck it bucket isn't new (people have been putting stuff in it for years!). However in this instance I was inspired by a Reddit/Weddit thread where couples listed all of the details and worries of weddings that they were going to ditch. My interpretation of the Bridechilla fuck it bucket is that it is a magical vessel where all of your wedding expectations, tasks, and unfinished DIY projects go.

The fuck it bucket comes in handy when disposing of the things that you initially thought were important, but six months (or six minutes) in, you realized aren't worth it. Traditions, expectations, trends, favors and well-intentioned DIY projects can all find a new home in the fuck it bucket.

REHEARSAL DINNERS

I come from a country (Australia) where pre-wedding rehearsal dinners aren't a thing, so I find the tradition a little perplexing. The money alone that goes into planning a rehearsal dinner can be pretty crazy; it's like a complete wedding in itself. Plus, the timing of the event – the night before the wedding kicks off – can be pretty intense. Wedding magazines like to paint the rehearsal dinner as a time to unwind and mingle, "Just have a great time. Have a drink. Have a little meal, and go back to your hotel and relax." Hearty congratulations to the 1% of couples who live in that world, but I'm guessing you'll probably be thinking about all the stuff you've still got to do, including shaving your legs, writing your speech, and redoing the seating chart for the 10th time.

I know this whole book is about being a Chilla and not being overwhelmed (and chill you will be), but I am also a realist. Even the most organized couples will have last minute shit to handle. Allowing yourself a little downtime, when you aren't "on", is a great way to prepare for your wedding day. That can be hard to do if you are hosting a party.

If you aren't keen on ditching the rehearsal dinner entirely, consider ways to tone it down. Have rehearsal drinks. Host a cocktail party with appetizers instead of a sit-down meal and then fuck off home and get some sleep. Don't feel pressured to plan a huge rehearsal dinner that goes on late into the night. Be flexible and open to making changes to this tradition.

DAY AFTER EVENTS

The day after party/brunch/lunch can be an excellent way to share some more time with your guests, but like many wedding-related events, it can also feel like an extra production. What used to be just, "Let's meet for a brunch or a BBQ," has turned into, "Let's plan a third wedding." Seriously, I've read wedding blogs and magazines touting day-after events that are fully catered with staff and fancy crockery – who has the time? If you are keen to host a day-after event but lack time and money to organize it, consider asking your in-laws or extended family to host the event (this is a great job to pass on, especially if they are keen to help). If you just want to call it a day at the end of your wedding and go home or off to a honeymoon somewhere delicious, then chuck the day-after events straight into the fuck it bucket and move on with your life.

PHOTO BOOTHS

Photo booths can be fun, but they can be massive duds. If you aren't hiring a photo booth company (who the hell would have imagined that would be a thing?), then you need to consider photo booth placement. Do you have props? How is the lighting? Are guests using their phone cameras or are you supplying one?

Who packs up the photo booth after the wedding? Will you ever look at the photo booth photographs again? Is the photo booth a distraction from the party, where everyone could be dancing instead of wearing novelty glasses and feather boas that fall apart before they are even out of the packet? These are questions that already, even writing this, make me edge towards the fuck it bucket.

GIFT BAGS

Let's all just stop this insanity now. We don't need gift bags. It's not the Oscars, it's your wedding. No one wants half the shit that people suggest you should put in wedding gift bags: a bottle of water, a muesli bar, one size fits all mono-grammed flip-flops and two tabs of aspirin. It's just stuff they've got to get rid of or leave in a hotel room for the maid to clean up and she's probably thinking, "Oh fuck, not another piece of shit wedding gift bag, give me strength, off to landfill for you, another thing clogging up this already desperately polluted planet." Then *she* throws it in the fuck it bucket. Save everyone the step and forget it.

HOTEL BLOCKS

To my mind, hotel blocking is very old-fashioned and can be overpriced compared to the deals you get online. If you are traveling overseas, or getting married in a location with one hotel, or at a location that books out very quickly, and you're concerned that people can't use the internet to book their accommodation, then I would suggest you connect them with good companies that help arrange hotel blocks. Otherwise, get it off the list. Look after yourself, and give people enough time and information, so they can go and book their own hotels. Throw hotel blocks into the fuck it bucket and watch them burn.

GIFTS, GIFTS, AND MORE GIFTS

One of my favorite things to diss are gifts. Gifts for the bride, gifts for the par-ents, gifts for the driver that drove you to the venue. I mean, we seem a little bit obsessed with giving people gifts. Don't get me wrong, I love gifts – I love receiv-ing gifts, I love giving gifts. But at the moment, we are going through a gift-giving renaissance. And the renaissance needs to end because the Bridechilla Commu-nity is swamped with messages from Chillas saying:

I don't know what to give this person as a gift.
I feel stressed about having to find a gift.

I haven't got time to think about a gift.
Do I need to give them a gift?
How much should I spend on the gift?
When should I give them the gift?
Do I need to give them a gift to say, "Would you be in my bridal party?"
Do I need to give them a gift to say, "Thanks for organizing"?

No! Stop it! Stop with the gifts. It stresses me out, man. And again, it's like the gift bag. The thought is lovely, but no one's going to judge you, or think any less of you, if you don't give them a special wine bottle with a personalized label that says "Will you be my bridesmaid?" plus another special box of perfume to say "Thank you for being my bridesmaid." A card, or something handwritten and delightful, is perfect and much more personalized and thoughtful, especially if you're on a budget. Excess gifts are in the fuck it bucket now.

THE GUESTBOOK

As a guest, I freaking hate the guestbook. I think, "Fuck, I've got to write something? I'm drunk. I haven't got time to think of something witty, and funny, that I will be judged for forever or until they throw the guestbook out." A lot of people seem to spend a lot of time worrying about the guestbook. What sort of book should it be? Should it have a fancy pen or will a biro suffice? Is the paper un-coated or coated, whatever the fuck that means?

I want you to do a little exercise. Ask a married friend how many times they have gone to that guestbook and looked at it since they got married. I'm not saying they're going to sit and read the guestbook every night, that would be weird, but after a quick post-wedding scan, I bet that book is going in a box in the garage. Then one day they will take that box to the dump, and then think, "What was in that box? Oh, it's our wedding guestbook! It's gone now forever. Oh well."

If you've got a guestbook, great. I just think that if it's a problem, or you feel stressed about having to find a guestbook, or finding something to write with, or write on, just forget it. Chuck it in the fuck it bucket. Or just print out a bunch of cool cards or buy some off Etsy, put them on a table, and then figure out what to do with them later — which will probably entail putting them in a drawer or a box and forgetting about them forever.

RECEPTION GAMES

Are we seven years old? When people suggest we play games at weddings, my immediate thought is "Why are we playing games at a wedding?" We should just be drinking, and talking and dancing. Don't feel like you need to fill the reception with activities. We're all adults. We know what a wedding is. We know how to look after ourselves. It's totally cool; we don't need games. Fill the bucket.

THE SEND-OFF

The end of wedding send-off is one of those things that as a guest I always feel a bit naff having to participate in. The send-off is something that a lot of old people love to do, the grand hurrah, and yes, I suppose it can be quite quaint. But also, I think it's a weird way to end a party.

Sometimes guests line up across from one another and raise their hands up together making a tunnel like they're in primary school. The couple runs through the tunnel, half-bending at the waist because the tunnel is never high enough. I have no fucking idea why an adult would choose to do this. As they pass through the tunnel, people yell at the couple, "Bye! Go and have sex now! Or don't, just go to sleep. Bye!"

Sometimes, instead of the line, it's a big circle, and the couple goes around and says goodbye to everyone. It's slow, and because I am cynical and by that time ordering the Uber, I don't really care for it. I'd rather wave from a distance to the happy couple and send them funny GIFs on WhatsApp than make tunnels out of my hands, but that's just me, and for that, I am throwing send-offs in the fuck it bucket.

CHAIR COVERS

Fuck them. They are ugly chair condoms that will eat up your money. No one is offended by naked chairs, and if they are, they need to think about their choices. I am more offended by shiny lycra chair covers with big bows than a naked chair. Chair covers are expensive and disgusting, and I passionately feel that they belong in the fuck it bucket.

BRIDESMAIDS' SHOES

Unless one bridesmaid is wearing steel-capped work boots without explanation while the rest of your bridal party is in stilettos, no one acknowledges bridesmaids' feet. The day is about you and your partner, and eating cake, drinking and dancing. Whether they match or not, no one cares, and if they don't match, no one will remember. It's just time to let matchy shoes go and put that concept in the fuck it bucket.

CAKE SERVERS

If you're spending your hard-earned money on special decorative cake servers, don't bother. No one cares, and you will never use them again. The fuck it bucket is where they live now.

DANCE LESSONS

Into the fuck it bucket. Who has time? I remember leaning over to Rich during dinner at our wedding saying, "Oh, shit. We were supposed to practice some dance," and he just said, "Let's wing it; let's improvise, it's our wedding." Which is just one of the many reasons why I married him.

We played an old school song ("Comin' Home Baby" by Mel Tormé), and we ended up just doing a bit of a made-up jive and when it got weird, quickly invited everyone to the dance floor.

If you want to do a six-year preparation for a surprise dance, more power to you. But I've barely got time to scratch myself, let alone go to dancing classes every week. Also, if you want to ditch the first dance altogether, I wholeheartedly support you on that too! Pre-prepared, complicated first dance routines can go straight in the fuck it bucket.

MATCHING "GETTING READY" ROBES

No doubt matching robes are pretty and perhaps they are nice gifts for brides-maids, but I just don't know if they're necessary. It's just more stuff to buy and store later on, plus, who wears robes IRL? Hugh Hefner (RIP), divorced women preparing for Tinder dates and people in hospital.

Certainly, no one is going to look at your wedding photos and think, "Oh my God, they're not wearing matching robes. What the hell is going on? Why aren't the bridesmaids and the bride wearing matching robes? What an absolute sham-ble!" I think they look pretty. Good on you if you've got them (and want to spend money on them). If not: fuck it bucket.

SPECIAL GLASSWARE

People seem obsessed with getting bride and groom, groom and groom, or bride and bride glassware for the day, and I just couldn't give a shit, honestly. It's not really a big deal. It's a fun little accessory to have, that you'll probably never use again or will probably leave at the venue by accident.

OTHER ELEMENTS AND TASKS TO PERHAPS CONSIDER FUCK IT BUCKETING:

ENGAGEMENT PICTURES

Unless these come in a package deal, you don't need them. Check Facebook, I am sure you have a bunch of great couple shots.

CUSTOM COCKTAILS

Booze is booze. They're fun, but a good vodka, lime and soda gets me just as excited as a custom job.

WEDDING SIGNS

In particular, the ridiculous, "Choose a seat and not a side" sign. What the fuck is that sign about anyway? If you can't be bothered to make them or to buy them, bye Felicia.

HAND-PAINTED SIGNS

I like to look at these on Pinterest but by golly, who has the time or access to weathered wood to make them?

FANCY NAPKINS

Specialty napkins and linens can look really lovely but they can also be really pricey. Ikea makes very nice paper napkins in great patterns and color ranges for a fraction of the price.

CAKE CUTTING

If gathering people to watch you cut a cake isn't on your bucket list, you know which bucket you can put this in.

RETURN ADDRESS STAMPS

There is no scientific proof that this will make people return RSVPs quicker, or even at all.

BRIDESMAID INVITES

Just ask them, with your mouth – or voice, you know what I mean. A great way to get them into the Bridechilla spirit is with our guide for bridesmaids, the *Maidchilla Manual*. I wrote that one too!

I hope the thing you take away from this chapter is that there are lots of details that are lovely to include in your wedding day preparations but to be honest they don't matter. We do, sometimes, disconnect a little bit from reality when planning this stuff, and think, "I need this. My event's not going to be good enough without it."

Every time you come across a decision like that, I want you to think about the events you've attended, whether it's a wedding or a party, and consider the moments that stood out to you. What do you remember? Why was it an awesome party? What were the details that were most important to you, at that moment? I'll bet they had nothing to do with matching glassware or robes. So, as you plan, embrace the fuck it bucket and the joy of disposing of expectations and useless crap!

BRIDECHILLA STEPS

> **Find things you don't want or need and put them in the fuck it bucket.**

you do you

A Bridechilla is somebody who, with the love of their life by their side, can conquer the wedding world one decision at a time.
They're decisive and strong.

Bridechilla Jess

The Guest List

THE GUEST LIST IS A CHALLENGE, I'm not going to lie. I'm all about reality, and for many couples, wedstress begins with choosing who is in and who is out. Perhaps you've had a crack at writing a draft guest list? Maybe you and your partner have written separate lists and when they are combined you realize you could fill a local football stadium? Maybe your partner has added 23 second cousins, none of whom you have met or care to meet for the first time on your wedding day! In this chapter, I'm going to help you polish your guest list, and by polish, I mean ditch a bunch of people who shouldn't be on your list in the first place. Sayonara bitches. When it comes to weddings, obligation appears in many forms. Sometimes it is connected to friends, sometimes to money and sometimes to how your inner circle of people feel you should do things. Often the most dramatic form of obligation that we get wrapped up in is the guest list.

Who you choose to invite, to have there to celebrate with you, is a big part of your wedding. No matter how large or small your wedding celebrations will be, creating the guest list can be one of the most emotionally challenging exercises in the whole wedding planning adventure. There are lots of deciding factors that surround creating a guest list: money, venue size, family expectations and what sort of vibe you want to create at your event. It can sometimes feel like a bit of a chicken-and-egg situation.

- Do you find a venue and then decide how many people you wish to attend your wedding?
- Do you start with a budget, then find a venue and then create your guest list?
- Do you make a preliminary guest list then create a budget and then find a venue?

Sheesh, what a mind fuck. I'm probably going to disappoint you here, but there's actually no magic answer. Your circumstances are unique, but there is one guiding force that I implore you to reflect upon, and that is eradicating the obligation wedding guest. Deviation from obligation can be scary, but also gosh darn exciting!

Before we get into the nitty-gritty of the guest list and who you can possibly ditch, let's do an imagination exercise. I'd say close your eyes, but because you are reading this that would be stupid! Ready?

OK. I want you to think about all of the weddings that you've attended. For how many of those weddings do you feel that perhaps you may have been an obligation guest? Perhaps you weren't on the A list. No judgment. It's a harsh question to ask but stay with me. Perhaps you attended a co-worker's wedding, or your second cousin's wedding, or the wedding of someone from college that you haven't seen for years. Of course they wanted you there, but perhaps you were on the B or even C list. Perhaps they invited you out of obligation.

I'd like you to think of the last time that you saw that co-worker, or that you had dinner or drinks with your second cousin. When did you last catch up with that college friend? When did you last have a one-on-one conversation? Remember the wedding day where you were that obligation guest. On that wedding day, how many minutes do you think you spent with the couple?

You drank a bit of their champagne, gave them a wave across the room. You might have had a quick catch up with the bride, an awkward squat next to the table, and said, "Hello. I love your dress! What have you been doing the last ten years?" "Oh, not much. Met this guy, had five jobs, my dog died and joined a cult! You?"

This is what can happen. People invite people from their past, who may not necessarily be a part of their future, because they feel obliged to do so. Perhaps the weddings where you may (or may not) have been an obligation guest were hosted by people who are loaded. Good for them! Perhaps they were members of the "bigger is better" wedding crew, the sort of people who invite a bunch of extended friends to their wedding so they can say, "We had 400 people at our wedding. It was amazing." Then great, I'm glad you went, and I hope you enjoyed yourself!

The purpose of that exercise wasn't to make you feel bad; I hope it's the opposite. Whether you intend to invite 40 people or 400, I'd like to help you make positive guest list choices for your wedding. Whether it is for financial reasons or you just need a kick in the butt and a bit of Bridechilla courage to say that perhaps these people aren't a big part of your lives anymore and you wouldn't miss them at your wedding, I'm going to help you out.

I am fully aware that family relationships are complicated. Friendships are complicated. Life is complicated! It can be a struggle when it comes to deciding who should be on your guest list without causing drama or breaking up families. But when you look back at your wedding photos, you'll want to feel good about them and hopefully remember everyone who was present. No one wants to think, "Who is that? I mean she's very familiar, but I just can't place her name? Is that someone you worked with?"

"Oh, yeah. It was at that weird software company, and you two got along really well for a couple of years. When did you last see her? Did she move to Spain?"

Of course, people come and go, and it's inevitable that some people you know now won't be your best friend in twenty years' time, but in planning your guest list, wouldn't it be great to prevent that weird peering at the photo moment in the future?

After that exercise, I'm hoping that there are a few people on your list that you realize are now potentially obligation guests. The one thing about being an obligation guest, and knowing that you're an obligation guest, is that you probably won't be that offended if you don't get invited in the first place. My top three obligation guests are:

THE CO-WORKER

Do you like your job and your work people? That's great! Will you be working there in five years? Do you see your co-workers socially (not just work drinks)? Have they met your partner? Do you know their partner? Do you like them as real friends and not just office friends who bonded over a mutual disdain for the boss?

If you do like one person but not the rest of the workplace, are you considering inviting the others so it's not awkward for you even though you don't like them as people? Why should these people share a day of joy with you and your closest friends? Because you want to avoid a moment of social discomfort?

PARENTS' FRIENDS

If your parents or your in-laws are wedding donors contributing money to your wedding and they're holding the guest list over your head, that's PGLB – Parental Guest List Blackmail. I call BS on PGLB. Let them have their own parties and invite Barry and Carol from tennis. If they want to see Lorraine, your third cousin once removed, then let them do it on their own time. As I mentioned previously, communication and honesty can go a long way in these circumstances.

- Ask them how important these extra guests are to them.
- What obligation do you have to these people that means they simply must be invited to your wedding?
- Are they on the list because your parents are trying to keep up with the Joneses? Do they want to show you off because you're fabulous?

That's all great. Rather than paying $300 to have them be at your wedding though, send them a nice card with a wedding photo instead and avoid having the bill and inviting virtual strangers! Solved.

Have the guest list conversation with your parents. Explain to them that you are hoping to have a more intimate and meaningful event, where the people who attend are really important to you and have meaning in your life. Work to get the message across without dissing their friends, but be firm enough to make sure they understand where you are coming from.

As a compromise, perhaps your parents would like to throw a pre- or post-wedding shower, dinner, or BBQ and invite all of their extended friends and family to celebrate with you? Give them options, let them be heard and then shut that shit down.

FRIENDS' PARTNERS YOU HAVE NEVER MET

Rich and I set a firm rule with our guest list, and that was no one was to be invited that hadn't met both of us. So if one of my friends hadn't met Rich, then too bad, they weren't coming to the wedding. We had fewer than fifty people at our wedding. The venue was stretched to capacity and in no way was this an easy task, BUT because we had defined the "rules" and both respected them and didn't bend them at all, it worked. The last thing we wanted to do was introductions on our wedding day. It's not a social mixer; it's your wedding. Of course, this rule is malleable, but it can save some drama if you stick to your guns.

Sure, some people, including family, were annoyed. I'll wear that, but for us, it worked and saved a lot of stress. It meant that the guests who were there on the day were our people. If you're having a small wedding and you can't stretch the numbers, even if the groom's best friend has met someone that he says is "the one," if you've never met them, let them have their third date at a restaurant, not at your wedding.

My final piece of advice on the guest list, the most important piece of information I can give you, is that you don't want to have anyone at your wedding that you have to pretend to be happy to see.

You shouldn't have to fake smile on your wedding day. You don't want to have to say, "Hi. It's so good to see you!" but deep down inside you're thinking, "I really resent you, and I don't want you here, but I have to because you're an obligation guest."

In the end, the guest list comes down to four points:

- How much money do you have?
- Who's in?
- Who's out?
- What are your obligations?

Like your budget, the guest list is going to need clear goals and guidelines. Have a conversation with your partner about who the non-negotiable guests are. Figure out what is the absolute maximum number of guests that you envisage attending your wedding. This is always fun.* Do you first work out your guest list and then your budget, or do you find a venue, work out the pricing and then the guest list? I suggest you create the list early on, preferably at the same time you calculate your budget. When you have the, "How much money are we comfortable spending on our wedding" talk, you should sit down together and write a draft guest list.

The first draft should include people who absolutely must be invited, such as immediate family and close friends. The people who you always imagined would be at your wedding and if they weren't you'd be devastated. Next on the list are friends, co-workers, and distant relatives.

Now you have a clear first draft. Unless money is no object or you have a large wedding venue (or culturally it's cool to invite everyone), cutting the list is inevitable.

Make an A and B list: A the "must invite" list and B the "maybe invite" list. I've talked a lot about A and B lists on the podcast and I really want to reiterate that putting people on the B list doesn't mean they are not as important to you or that they don't have value in your lives. Perhaps your venue only holds 50 people and you have 100 on your list, or your budget will only cover 30 people, and you have 400 people on your list (sucks to be you, sorry). The guest list is as much circumstantial as it is emotive. When looking at your draft guest list:

- Are there names on the list that you don't recognize or people you hardly know?
- Why are these people on your list?

- What do you gain by having them attend one of the most intimate and per-sonal moments of your life?
- If I came along and removed them from the list, how would you feel?
- Does your list contain suggestions from parents and in-laws?

If you are paying for and organizing your wedding, then it is totally up to you who is invited. Fact. If you haven't seen a friend in years, cut them free. If you don't know their kids' names or have their current address, maybe Skype them to catch up, but inviting them to your wedding might be a bit much. Just because you rekindled a friendship on Facebook doesn't mean they get to come to your wedding.

Weddings aren't about onus. They are about you and your partner...and cake. As with all big decisions, the guest list should be worked on together. It's a team exercise. Go through the pros and cons of who you want there, and work it out together. Write the list and leave it for a few days or a few weeks. Don't feel pres-sured to make decisions quickly. Think about all the reasons listed in this chapter why you might invite or not invite someone. Picture the day and who you want to be there to celebrate. If anyone is being a jerk about not being invited, send them my way!

BRIDECHILLA STEPS

> **Lock in your budget before creating your guest list.**
> **Create an A and B list.**
> **Don't invite people out of obligation.**
> **Guests should be in your future and not just from your past.**
> **Don't invite anyone that you have to pretend to be happy around.**

* Sarcasm

exhale the bullshit

Being a Bridechilla is about handling things in your own way based on your priorities as a couple. It's about not letting society or tradition dictate what you do. It's about throwing a rockin' party that represents your and your partner's relationships, interests, and values. It is about getting educated and handling issues that come up with grace so you don't stress out too much!

Bridechilla Erica

Hired Help

Wedding planners and coordinators

IN MY DAY JOB AS A TV PRODUCER, I organize and negotiate with people and locations. I also create schedules, interview contributors and delve deep to find the best story to tell. Part of my job is to ensure that the outcome of a show is exactly what we planned for. Of course, nothing goes "perfectly," so the other part of my job is having enough backup plans to fix shit when it goes wrong, which happens pretty often. I enjoy my work (mostly), but the pressure of making television compared to the pressure of planning a wedding is very different. So for me, planning an event for 50 people with what seemed like a million moving pieces was a whole new game.

Organizing, planning, making lists, color coding, worrying about lists, bartering, schmoozing, reorganizing lists (and writing more lists!), isn't everyone's idea of fun. Many people, in fact, do not like doing the aforementioned things and would rather pay a professional to avoid them altogether. If that's you, I say DO IT!

One of the big secrets to being an instant Bridechilla and Groomchilla is to know your limitations, and to value your time and your money. I often use the example of craft and DIY projects. There are plenty of people who take pleasure in devoting four weekends in a row to using hot glue guns and learning the art of folding ten thousand Japanese origami cranes and decorating a warehouse wedding space. But there are also plenty of people who say, "No fucking way. Absolutely not. Get the damn glue gun away from my good rug; it's dripping and messy! I wouldn't be caught dead folding a credit card statement let alone ten thousand fucking cranes."

Knowing which type of person you are will make your wedding planning choices a whole lot easier. Figuring out how hands-on you want to be, and what you are happy to outsource and delegate, will change your wedding planning life. You may decide that you want to go it completely alone, or you may consider hiring a wedding planner.

When I used to think about wedding planners, my mind jumped to the wonderful and kooky Franck Eggelhoffer (Martin Short) from the movie *Father of the Bride*. Franck is a lovable prick that nearly sends the father, George (played by Steve Martin), to an early grave with his excessive spending and over the top antics, "I vill go talk to Honk. Now, we don't want to lose him. Hiss a genius and we need his maaaaand!"

He's fun but also pushy, and although I would question his business ethics, he's persuasive, and the wedding did look pretty fab in the end. Who cares if George was headed to bankruptcy weeks after Annie's wedding?! I do not doubt that people like Franck exist, but from my experience, most wedding planners are pretty down to earth, realistic humans who in many situations save couples money and time rather than overcharging them.

WEDDING PLANNER

A wedding planner is generally seen as the full-service option – my words not theirs! They are with you from early on in your wedding planning and can hold your hand and guide you through major planning decisions and details. They can help you create a detailed time line and budget and pick out your venue and vendors. They will also help you negotiate contracts, organize rehearsal dinners and book brunches and other wedding-related activities. Their team will ensure that your wedding day runs smoothly, overseeing all the details that you shouldn't be thinking about on the day. Some planners will offer partial planning, which is perhaps bordering on wedding coordination. Most wedding planners charge a flat fee, but some do offer a percentage fee, usually between 10-20% of your total budget.

WEDDING COORDINATOR

Wedding coordinators are the clever people who take all your wedding research and quotes and turn them into wedding reality. They are a lighter version of a wedding planner, guiding you through the latter part of your wedding planning leading up to your wedding day. I advise you to connect with a wedding coordinator several months before your wedding to go over your wedding time line, guest list, and vendor and venue details. This way, your coordinator can oversee the creation of your wedding schedule and can go through all the things you might have missed. Coordinators confirm bookings, can assist with seating charts, timings, work with on-site managers at your venue, and just like wedding planners, they can be there to oversee and run your wedding day.

The decision to hire a wedding planner or coordinator may be a simple one. If you have a busy job and know that making sneaky calls and emails during the day to vendors and suppliers might get you fired, then perhaps hiring a wedding planner would be a good option. The same goes if you feel completely overwhelmed/disinterested/sweaty about wedding planning, that also might be a good indicator to begin exploring your wedding planner options.

Hiring a wedding planner can come at varying stages of planning. Some couples hire a planner before they have made any major decisions, others wait until three weeks before the wedding. If you are thinking about engaging the services of a planner, I recommend inviting them to help you as soon as you can. Before you hit the interwebs and start your planner search, I suggest you go back to your budget and consider how much money you can afford to allocate to pay for a wedding planner or coordinator.

This is not to say that you will magically find your dream planner within your budget immediately, but like all expenses, it's silly going out and taking meetings at The Ritz, when you are more likely to have a motel budget (hey, don't we all!). Be realistic, but not a tight-ass. You get what you pay for! Jenny, who says that she will plan your wedding for a $300 flat rate, probably has a heart of gold and pockets full of "life experience," but if she has never planned a wedding, she may not be the top of the list for your wedding planning needs. Your ideal wedding planner or coordinator is the sort of person that won't flinch if you throw a tennis ball at their face. I don't recommend you actually do that though. That would be very rude.

Wedding coordinators and planners have balls of steel. They can re-hem a dress with a toothpick and can talk your mother-in-law out of a panic attack when she sees the maid of honor's thigh tattoo. As well as superior organizational skills, coordinators and planners have enthusiasm and bags of experience using their poker face to cover up potential disasters, which they fix without you ever being aware that there was a disaster in the first place. They are wedding superheroes. Bow down to them, bow down.

When you hire a wedding planner and coordinator, you are gaining all of their magic contacts. Their vendor lists are people that they work with regularly, trust and rely upon. Their knowledge and contacts are their business, and using those connections to ensure everything works and goes to plan is what they do best.

Your planner wants you to have an excellent day without worry or stress. Wedding planners and coordinators are Bridechilla nurturers, just like me! They are the ones who panic when the flowers don't show up on the morning of the wedding, not you. If the icing on the cake is green instead of white or there are no chairs for your guests to sit on during the ceremony, it's their problem to fix; that's why you are paying them. Wedding planners and coordinators are lateral thinkers, counselors, and drill sergeants. They get shit moving; they make things happen. Wedding planners and coordinators will also:

- Add details to the day that you might have missed (or not even thought of).
- Give you an alternative perspective and keep you up-to-date with current and future wedding trends.
- Produce design elements to create a personalized look.
- Coordinate the florist, caterer, printers, graphic designers, transportation and any other additional vendors.
- Help you create table settings and decor, lighting and other audiovisual details.
- Advise on possible entertainment, timing and extra details that you may never even think of.
- Meet vendors and deliveries, and handle any no-shows.
- Solve last-minute emergencies.
- Set up and check the ceremony and reception spaces and deal with any weather issues, e.g., moving an outdoor ceremony if it is raining.
- Make sure that the wedding party is running to schedule and are in the right places at the right time.
- Coordinate the reception time line with the venue, caterers, entertainment and MCs.
- Collect all of your items, wedding gifts and leftover wedding cake (don't forget the cake!) and make sure they get back to you safely.
- Return all rentals and borrowed items and sign off all suppliers' pickups.
- Ensure that the venue space is left clean and that your deposits are returned.

Experienced wedding planners and coordinators are sassy oracles who should know everyone in the business. They keep up-to-date with what's new, who sucks, where someone got food poisoning last week, and who drives a hard bargain. They are your main gal or guy. They should be able to do everything from helping you find the ideal wedding ceremony location to the extra little touches you may not have considered. They should use their prowess, their contacts, and their know-how to get you the best prices and those extra special inclusions. Vendors they recommend should be within your limitations, and if they aren't, they will usually go out and find one that is.

I have heard some amazing stories of wedding planners and coordinators saving the day when it comes to wedding fiascoes, and the beautiful thing is most of the couples involved in these situations had no idea that these crises were even occurring.

You wouldn't go to Uncle Bob to get your teeth fixed (unless he is a dentist of course), so be sure to do your research – read reviews and ask for client feedback and testimonials when choosing your wedding planner or coordinator. You are going to want to like this person. You don't have to be BFFs, but you need to have faith that they are up to the task and that you will get along with them enough to be in contact with them pretty regularly during your wedding planning.

QUESTIONS FOR WEDDING PLANNERS OR COORDINATORS

- What are some of the challenges they have faced?
- Can they work with your budget? Is it realistic? Ask them for some feedback on your expectations for the day.
- What are some of the ways they would suggest to save money and still have an awesome day?
- How much time will they commit to planning your wedding?
- How often will you be in contact in the lead-up to the wedding?
- What if you don't gel with their suppliers? How negotiable are they?
- Will they use your preferred suppliers or will they use their own?
- Are they affiliated with any venues?
- What is their favorite wedding or event that they have planned?

You should see your wedding planner or coordinator as a very business-oriented friend, someone that you trust, someone that you feel comfortable being honest and open with, and someone who you are happy to hand over your wedding budget to, knowing that shit is going to get done. Like any wedding vendor, if it doesn't feel right, if you don't feel like they fit the above criteria, then move on and find someone who does. Don't settle for someone who is a bit cheaper but you feel might not be as reliable.

MY VENUE COMES WITH A COORDINATOR, ISN'T THAT THE SAME THING?

If you have chosen to get married in a place such as a hotel or function center (winery, golf course), then most likely you will be provided with an in-house wedding coordinator that will be able to help you from the get-go. This is nice, but (surely you knew there was a *but* coming), often their services aren't on the same level of personalization as a hired wedding coordinator. It's good to remember that the in-house coordinator is probably handling a hundred other functions at that venue and yes, they are here to help you, but be mindful that your event a year in the future might not be top of mind every day for them. Hiring your own coordinator to work on the more personal details is a fantastic compromise, and they can additionally work with your venue coordinator to lock in the details connected to the day.

ASK FOR HELP

Weddings are huge events to organize and even if you know exactly what you want and you think you can handle it, don't be too proud to take on the help of others to get the job done. You don't want to be super-stressed and on the edge of a breakdown by the time your wedding day comes along. No matter how small the job, whether it is picking up flowers or dropping off dry cleaning, take the opportunity to assign people jobs. Create a spreadsheet or a shared document that you can email to family and friends. Ask for their availability and be clear about what you need them to do. It's better to over-explain than under-explain.

Don't rely on family and friends to do professional tasks. Too often things go awry when people try and save money by offsetting jobs to friends or family members and when they aren't done properly, shit hits the fan. Of course Aunty Jen, who has never made a four-tiered wedding cake potentially, might run into some issues with structural stability on a summer's day! Don't create more work for yourself (or those around you), think strategically about your helper choices and go professional wherever you can.

KEEP ORGANIZED

Use the *Bridechilla Field Guide* to keep track of your wedding planning info.

BRIDECHILLA STEPS

> **Ask to see examples of previous weddings that the coordinator has planned.**
> **Ask for references from the coordinator's past clients.**
> **Use a shareable document system to keep up to date with plans, schedule, and contacts.**
> **If you aren't using a wedding planner, allocate jobs to friends and family but don't rely on them for professional tasks. Rely on professionals instead. As Red Adair said, "If you think it's expensive to hire a professional to do the job, wait until you hire an amateur."**

you are as emotionally
stable as an Ikea table

A Bridechilla is a bride who is willing to accept that this one day of your life is not the be-all and end-all, but rather a moment to celebrate love, family, and friendship and therefore can relax and not sweat the small stuff.

Bridechilla Jaime

Quotes & Contracts
The business end of weddings

BRIDECHILLAS AND GROOMCHILLAS AREN'T CHEAPOS. As we've already deduced, you understand value and what is important to you. You know what you want and how much you are willing to pay for it and if you don't, you will by the end of this book. When you start the wedding quote process, you may lose your shit and potentially the will to live, or at least the will to get married. People are going to quote you high prices that make you want to move to a farm, disconnect the internet, and go completely off-grid forever.

Some vendors will put you in a "waiting for response" holding pattern, leaving you in limbo for weeks waiting for quotes. Which is ridiculous because surely they want your business?!

Some vendors will not be available for three years.

Some vendors will be shady or mysterious about prices altogether

Some vendors will send you a very long and involved questionnaire that feels like homework.

You must stay calm. You must get creative. You must carry on. Do it for me. Don't give up. Getting crazy quotes is an annoying rite of wedding planning passage that we all go through. It's annoying because you've probably burned time chasing the vendor and maybe even got your hopes up that they would fit into your budget; however, in an industry where prices can differ wildly for no particular reason, you've just got to move on and find a supplier who suits you and your budget. Receiving quotes that are way out of your budget can be a total kick in the guts. You are excited to be making plans, you've stalked them on Instagram and decided that you're picking up what they are putting down and then...bam. Millionaire's quote.

Rich and I received five quotes for catering for our wedding. We had a self-cater venue, a private property an hour out of the city which required the caterer to set up a kitchen on site. Side note: I adore self-catering venues but please for the love of the wedding Gods, don't assume that they will always be the cheaper option. Especially if you are required to provide facilities such as a kitchen, porta-ble refrigerator, and portaloos, additions can add up. The catering quotes for our wedding ranged from $5,000 to $21,000. For us, the highest quote of $21,000 was extreme. Put-your-glasses-on-to-see-if-you've-read-it-correctly extreme. We valued great food, local produce, and service...but not $21,000 worth of value, produce, and service! To be honest, the $21,000 quote company was more about "creating artisanal experiences and blah blah blah." They were "food designers" and are now very popular on Instagram, but we didn't want a Condé Nast spread, we wanted amazing, memorable food that would fill the bellies of our guests and put a smile on their dial.

Of course, as Instagram tells me, there are a lot of people who would have snatched up that $21,000 quote and good for them and all of their money! For us, it wasn't worth going back to negotiate and discuss quote flexibility because we knew they weren't going to budge as much as we would have needed them to even to get them to the property, let alone serve our guests food.

I am a big fan of utilizing wedding planners and coordinators; they are the key to helping you save money and connecting you with other vendors in your price range who share your plans and outlook for your wedding. Until we started receiving quotes back, we had no idea which quotes were reasonable and which were crazy. If we had an experienced planner or coordinator to contact and ask for feedback, we would have saved time and many, "You've got to be kidding?" eye rolls.

WHEN ASKING FOR QUOTES

Be mindful that many vendors are sole traders and during busy times their re-sponses can be a little slower. There has been an improvement in the industry over the past few years with vendors putting communication systems in place, hiring VAs to respond to inquiries and even better, being open and transparent about their prices on their websites. Like any wedding planning relationship, you want to feel confident that the people you hire understand your needs, budget, and time frame. If you don't vibe with them, or feel like they aren't getting it, look elsewhere. You don't have to be BFFs, but you do have to be confident in their skills and output. If they take four weeks to respond to an email or their testimo-nials aren't up to scratch with what you had hoped, move on.

- Be as specific as possible. Dates, times, hours needed, etc. (even if approxi-mate). The more info, the better.
- Dot point what you are asking them to do and when.

- Be clear and concise. They don't need your life story but they do need the basics of what you require.
- If you have any special requirements, tell them. Don't assume they will know.

- Before you start initiating relationships with vendors and asking for quotes, make sure you have a template set up to record the figures when they come in and a folder or spreadsheet ready to store the information.
- Pick three vendors in each category and start from there.
- There is no point in initially emailing 25 photographers. This is how people get overwhelmed with wedstress very quickly. They throw a bunch of emails out there and then start to panic when things come back way over budget, or they all come back within budget and you are spoilt for choice.
- Make sure that you look at testimonials, Yelp reviews, Google feedback, etc. Do your research and don't be hesitant to ask for more testimonials or to speak to a recent client about the services that they received.
- Know when it is appropriate to negotiate prices and when it's easier to walk away. For example, we negotiated to provide our own appetizers and dessert table. Our caterer agreed to this, which saved us a bunch of money. They were cool, but a lot of caterers would have told us to shove it.
- Be mindful that vendors are running businesses and have set their pricing to levels that they find fair for their services. Not everyone price matches. Trust your instinct with pricing. If it feels too good to be true or you get a whiff of shadiness, then move on. Find someone else.

CONTRACTS: READ THEM BEFORE YOU SIGN THEM, DERR

Don't scan through this section like I scan through iTunes agreements! Seriously, they could own all of our future children at this point, and I wouldn't know. Once you have decided that a vendor is for you, it's important to get your agreement in writing. Until you sign a contract and put down a deposit, you have no guarantees that vendors will hold the date of your wedding.

No matter how small the business, a contract should be signed. This is a Bridechilla non-negotiable. A contract is valuable for both parties in the agreement. It is so you know what the vendor will be supplying to you and when, and how much you will pay them to do so. A contract makes sure that both parties are aware of their rights and obligations via a written agreement. It will dictate what will occur in the case of cancelation, whether that entails a refund or an obligation on your behalf to pay the vendor regardless. A contract is just as important to the client as it is to the vendor, and if you come across a vendor who says "I'm not big enough to have a contract," or "I can't afford a lawyer to draw one up for me," I call bullshit.

There are thousands of results for "contract template" in a Google search. It is simple to download one and edit it as required. Yes, if you are a vendor, ideally it would be good have someone with some sort of legal qualifications to check it, but a basic contract isn't complicated and at a bare minimum should cover the points below:

- Dates and times of all services required, including the date of the wedding.
- Names of all parties involved in the agreement – even if you have wedding donors paying, the contract is between you and the vendor.
- The deposit and final payment amounts as well as the payment schedule.
- Contingency plans, e.g., what happens if it rains? Will your venue provide you with an alternative space or is it up to you?
- Description of services.
- Refunds and cancelation clauses.
- Ownership – particularly when it comes to photography. Discuss social media rights and whether they use images from your wedding for promotion, etc.
- Additional charges and taxes. Is the price final? Can you add extra people to the catering bill? How much will that cost?
- Rental items, what are the costs to you if damage is incurred or items are lost?

Don't sign anything until you have had time to read it – properly! If you have questions and amendments, make them known. Both you and the vendor should sign and date two copies. As always, if you don't feel comfortable signing any document or agreement, don't do it. If someone is pressuring you to agree to something and you need time to read it and reflect, take the contract away and take your time. If you are working with a wedding planner or coordinator, they will often oversee contracts and agreements on your behalf, but you are still required to read and sign.

BRIDECHILLA STEPS

> **Ensure a contract is in place for all services.**
> **Read and understand the contracts you sign.**
> **Seek legal counsel.**

The information provided in this book is intended to serve as general information and guidance. Legal advice must be tailored to the specific circumstances of each case, and this shouldn't be substituted for the advice of competent legal counsel.

progress not perfection

Bridechillas and Groomchillas are well-read and want to make educated decisions. Technology has helped us to see that it is okay to feel the way we feel, that there are others out there feeling the same way, whether it is having this really big wedding or something really simple – or nothing at all – it's okay!

Bridechilla Viviana

Venue, Food & Booze

WEDDINGS CAN TAKE MANY DIFFERENT SHAPES, formal, traditional, religious, casual, huge, minimalistic, vintage-inspired, *Game of Thrones* themed (perhaps not "Red Wedding" though!). The list is as long as your imagination. There are no rules. Especially in Bridechilla-land.

Your wedding is your gig, your main event, and sometimes the freedom to do whatever the heck you want can be overwhelming. After spending some time on Pinterest, with all the images and inspiration, it can easily feel like there is too much choice and have you wishing for the simplicity of the 1950s when everyone got married at a church, country club, or golf course.

Choosing a wedding venue, or venues, is a big decision and one that will shape all your plans to come, so it's not one to make in haste. However, let me remind you that it's just a place and wherever you choose to get married will be special because it's about you, not a ballroom or a view.

By now, I am hoping that you have shared your expectations for your wedding day with each other. These responses will help you home in on a style of venue that will fit your budget and your vision for your wedding. It will make the search for a venue and the decisions, like what kind of food and alcohol you would like to serve, that much easier.

LOCATION LOCATION

The location of your wedding, the venue, will not only help shape your day, but it will also dictate a lot of budget and practical decisions, like guest list, decor, theme and transportation.

Perhaps you are hoping to get married locally and have attended a wedding or function at a location that you believe would be ideal for your celebrations. Or perhaps you've bookmarked a dozen potential venues and are ready to jump into site visits. Before you move forward there are a couple of key factors that you should consider, such as:

- How many guests can you fit in the venue and how much will it cost?
- What time can you arrive and leave, including set up and pack down?
- Are there noise restrictions?
- Can you bring a caterer, or must you use in-house people?
- How easy is it to get guests to the venue? Do you need to use their vendors?
- Before you visit any venue, consider your wants and needs list.
- Think practically as well as aesthetically. For example, will you require wheel-chair access?
- Are you looking to hire somewhere that is relatively self-sufficient such as an all-inclusive venue?
- Is it important to you to include cultural traditions, and if so, can the venue cater to these requests?

PICK A DATE RANGE

After you have locked in your budget (you have locked it in, yes?), the next step in choosing your venue is having a date range in mind. I say range because in many situations flexibility is your friend. The time of the year that you plan to hold your wedding may be a deciding factor for where you choose to get married. Some popular venues are booked out up to three years in advance during peak spring and summer wedding season. Peak wedding time is like wedding kryptonite; when it's busy, your negotiating superpowers and flexibility diminish dramatically and for many venues the chance of booking a weekend wedding can be very unlikely.

Think resourcefully, if you have your heart set on a venue that is out of your budget in peak wedding time, inquire about off-peak or low season options. You may be surprised at how many sites will work for your business when they need it in the quieter months. Remember if you don't ask, they might not offer.

GET IN THE MOOD

When considering venues, imagine what sort of mood you want to create on your wedding day. Do you envisage a romantic, classic service in a ballroom deco-rated with roses, a string quintet, and champagne? (Sounds posh!) Or a barefoot beach wedding with fire drums, cocktails and a calypso band? Perhaps a mini-malist inner-city warehouse with a balloon canopy is more your style? Finding a location that can work realistically with your wedding vision is the first step in making it happen. Be open-minded but not decor delusional. Seeing an empty art gallery as a blank canvas is great, but if you wish to transform the blank canvas into something magnificent, you are probably going to need help from someone that has the time, money, and skills to make it happen. Have you the time? Have you the skills? If not, can you afford to pay someone who does?

If you are working with a wedding planner or coordinator, they will be able to assist you with design and decor and provide quotes for what you may need to add to venues to bring your vision to life. Planners and coordinators may be available to attend site visits with you and also give you feedback on your plans, particularly if they have worked at that venue before.

CONSIDER ALTERNATIVE VENUES

One of the most exciting things about choosing a wedding venue these days is variety. There are so many venues available now that would not have been consid-ered venues five years ago, and there are lots of companies that work on behalf of site owners to negotiate rental for events, like Airbnb for commercial properties.

Non-traditional venues are a great option for couples who want to make their own choices every step of the way, to have control of all facets of the planning process and to have the flexibility and freedom to bring in all of their suppliers of choice without the restrictions of a traditional venue.

Often when choosing a non-traditional venue, the result is an experience that you can truly identify with. If you're an artist, you can get married in a gallery, a chef in a culinary space, a historian in a landmark building. With an alternative space also comes the option to direct the flow of the event in an alternative way – why not eat, dance, and do the ceremony later?!

If you look past traditional wedding reception venues, country clubs and ho-tels, you will find that your community is filled with potential wedding venues. Warehouses, art galleries, private homes, listed properties, and local historical societies are options worth exploring when looking for wedding reception and ceremony locations. It's surprising how many of these venues are available to hire. Many historical and estate homes are government or state-owned, and to inquire about the availability of such sites is simply a matter of calling your local council or checking their website for a list of venues for hire.

For example, in my hometown of Hobart, Australia, the Hobart City Council owns art galleries, historic homes, waterfront piers, halls, old timber mills, the town hall, and some former churches that can be hired for private functions. These venues are available at reasonable rates ($100 to $500 per day) and many of which are in fabulous locations on the Hobart waterfront. Most of the venues have commercial kitchens or areas where a caterer could set up a temporary kitchen and bathrooms.

Be mindful when considering alternative venues that you are probably just hiring the space. You will need to provide everything for the venue, including tables, chairs, crockery, additional lighting, etc., all of which can be arranged by an event hire company or your planner or coordinator. However, these will come at additional cost and should be factored into your budget. Although you may be getting a venue for cheaper, the logistical components, set up time and rental costs may increase your budget substantially. In your venue search, try to disregard the stereotypes of what you think your wedding "should" be. Think outside the venue box and consider venues that aren't your standard wedding fare.

If you are considering hiring an alternative wedding venue, then be sure to always disclose the intended use of the property to the owners. Not revealing that you are using a property for a wedding or event can be problematic for all. If you aren't forthcoming with information or omit details, it may void your contract. To avoid potential drama and unnecessary stress, use alternative venue search websites like Splacer.co to find properties that are ready to host your event.

I featured a couple on *The Bridechilla Podcast* who had their reception at a retro hairdressing salon. They weren't hairdressers, but they loved the vibe, color and energy of the building. They used shampoo stations as a bar, filling the basin with ice and had a cocktail style reception, so their guests mingled around the cutting stations. It was fun and memorable, and with the help of their wedding planner, they were able to work within the confines of bumping in and out of the premises after business hours, so the hairdressers didn't miss any time. They had caterers bring food on site that was prepared in their nearby kitchen. This unique venue made for some pretty amazing and unexpected wedding photos.

WHAT IS INCLUDED WITH YOUR VENUE HIRE?

When booking any venue, make sure you are clear on what is provided in the initial hire of the venue and what details may be provided at an additional charge. Some questions you should ask a before signing the contract:

- How many guests can the venue accommodate?
- Are there other alternative dates available?
- Do they have different pricing structures and options?

- Are there additional charges for staying longer than the allocated time?
- Are there any additional fees – cleaning, staff, security?
- Can you bring your own cake or dessert table?
- If they have accommodation, can they provide discounted room blocks for your bridal party and guests?
- Is the hire fee for the use of the location alone or does it include extras?
- What are their rules of hire?
- Can you bring your own alcohol?
- Do they have preferred vendors that you are required to use?
- Is there flexibility in set up times? (If they have events the day before, what is the earliest time your coordinator can get access to the venue to set up?)

As always, ask questions and get all agreements and details in writing. With the popularity of peak season and the demand for venues comes the pressure on couples to make fast, on the spot decisions. Couples can feel rushed and panicked. They pay deposits even though they haven't fully decided. Like all big decisions in this process, I advise you to pencil your date in and sleep on it. Give yourself a moment to read the contract, think about logistics, timing, and budget. If you feel pressured in any way, ask for thinking time and if the venue is unwilling to give this to you, take a step back and breathe. There are plenty more fish in the Bridechilla venue sea.

SELF-CONTAINED VENUES

A self-contained venue is where you can hold both the ceremony and reception at the same location. They can be excellent for cutting back on transport and venue hire costs and negating the need to move your guests (and you) from one location to another. Using a self-contained venue can also save you money by avoiding doubling up on site fees for two locations.

The logistics of your wedding day are also something to consider when venue hunting. Is the venue photogenic? Will there be somewhere nice to have post-ceremony photographs while your guests enjoy drinkies and canapés without you having to abandon the party for an age to move to another location?

GETTING HITCHED OUTSIDE

Outdoor weddings can be great fun. Gorgeous views, fresh air, and sunshine... which all sounds great as long as the sun is out but also isn't cooking everyone, and the wind behaves itself, and the clouds and rain stay away.

We, although wonderful and powerful beings, have yet to figure out how to control the weather. It is one area that a wedding planner, the local weatherman/woman, and the Bureau of Meteorology can work hard to predict, but until the day of your wedding, it can be risky not knowing what sort of weather will come your way.

Hoping that it will be nice weather to get you through isn't a solid backup plan. Getting married outside is great as long as you have a tidy plan B to fall back on. If your venue doesn't have a backup indoor space, hiring a marquee is an option, but it is not always budget friendly. Marquees can only be erected on certain surfaces, and there will need to be time allocated for set up and take down.

If you need to hire a marquee, you will need to organize the booking in advance. They will give you a cut-off time for delivery and installation, so once that baby is booked, you pay for it. Unlike a hall or gallery, marquees will need to have power and water nearby for lighting and catering purposes, and if you are getting hitched away from bathrooms, portaloos will also be necessary. Be aware of the possibility of intruders such as insects and other people! If your ceremony is taking place in a public park, you may attract onlookers and rubberneckers.

When considering an outdoor location, also listen – is there road noise? Bird sounds? Traffic? Will any of these noises get in the way of your guests hearing the ceremony? Remember you will need to get permission to use any public outdoor area and possibly pay a fee to the local council. They can also give you a heads up on noise restrictions and whether you can cordon off an area ahead of time.

ALL-INCLUSIVE WEDDING PACKAGES

An all-inclusive package at a hotel, resort, or function center may suit your needs if planning and managing every detail of the event isn't an option for you (or isn't of interest), and you have a limited budget (although big fancy venues also offer all-inclusive packages, so it's not always the budget option!).

Most hotels and full-service wedding venues can provide you with package options, which will include everything you need to hold a function: food, beverages, staffing and venue hire. Destination weddings are an example of how all-inclusive packages can be a time saver if you aren't located near where you are getting married. Working with a resort or venue to select a package might suit you more than starting from scratch from afar.

Sometimes all-inclusive packages are given a bad name by being labeled as "cookie cutter" events. I've got two things to say about that:

1. Screw those guys and their opinions.
2. Packages can be very affordable, and any sign of "same same" can be swiftly

removed by personalizing your decor and adding touches of "you" all over the place.

It's your day, have it your way. No matter whether you are holding your reception in a hotel dining area or an inner-city warehouse, by focusing on smaller details and touches you can make any venue shine.

RETURN TO YOUR VISION

Thinking about the timing of your celebration and what sort of food and atmosphere you want will help guide your venue decision. Weddings do not have to be formal, seated affairs with alternate drop meals followed by speeches and dancing. If that format doesn't work for you, ditch it. You can get married at a bowling alley with sushi and a silent disco. I repeat, there are no rules.

If you picture a relaxed event where guests mingle, and there is no formal seating, then perhaps a ballroom isn't the location for you, or perhaps it is, minus the big round tables? Venues are malleable to some extent, but if you do have grand plans to push the limits of their use, then make sure you discuss them with the venue owner or manager to make sure that your visions can become a reality and you aren't signing up to a venue that won't embrace what you are hoping to create.

COCKTAIL PARTY RECEPTIONS

If you fancy mingling with your guests and not doing as much formal sitting and eating, not to mention getting everyone on the dance floor sooner rather than later, a cocktail reception can be a good option.

One misconception about cocktail-style events is that your guests will be hungry. Many substantial dishes can be served cocktail-style, and they don't have to be finger food and bite sized hors d'oeuvres that leave you hungry ten minutes later. Talk to your venue or caterer about what they recommend and, again, get creative.

If you are considering a cocktail-style function, think about the food that you are serving and how easy it is to eat in a non-formal environment, e.g. standing whilst holding a drink. This is one of my pet peeves of cocktail events. If I am supposed to be holding a plate and utensils and a drink, I am missing one arm. Cocktail does not equal no seats or tables. Guest comfort is important so be sure to pre-plan seating and eating area options.

Food truck weddings are one version of a cocktail-style event, where your guests have lots of options for fun food to eat. For more substantial food that keeps within the cocktail reception boundaries, set up a range of self-service food stations. Noodle bars, paella, burger, or curry stations are a way to add diversity to the food service.

Choosing to make your reception a little more casual doesn't mean you have to forgo traditional formalities such as speeches, cake cutting, and the first dance – schedule them in! But if you're opting for a cocktail function because you want to avoid conventional customs, don't go nuts.

THINK ABOUT SPACE AND SEATING

Whether you are choosing to have a seated dinner or a cocktail event, be mindful of providing enough seating for your guests to be comfortable, particularly for the older folk and those who chose to wear fabulous but spine shattering footwear. The traditional ratio is to have enough seats for about a third of your guests, made up of bar stools, regular chairs, and armchairs scattered around. Nanna and your stiletto-wearing friends will thank you!

SHARED TABLES: THE NEW BUFFET

If a cocktail reception feels a little casual and you wish to have your guests seated for meal service, you may want to consider shared plates. A homely and generous way to serve food (but still less expensive and more inventive than giving everyone the same dish) is with shared platters. Each table is served a selection of vegetables, salads, and bread, or antipasto platters and main meals that they can serve themselves. It's very Mediterranean and can look spectacular if presented well. One caterer I spoke to recently said that shared platters are just "fancy buffets," but they are also the most popular choice on their menu. Staffing is lower as they don't have to plate and deliver hundreds of meals and menus can be more exotic and inventive. Guests also feel like they are in control of portion sizes and they appreciate getting a choice without having to line up at a buffet.

We chose this option for our wedding and were delighted with the results. Our caterer used clever ways to present the food at different heights on the table (using stands and even vintage spindles), and they had some eclectic bowls and crockery that very much suited our venue.

CHAMPAGNE AND CAKE RECEPTION

Head back to the sixties with a champagne and cake reception. This is exactly what it sounds like. Instead of serving a three-course meal, you can make your wedding an afternoon affair with a table of gorgeous cakes and a healthy selection of champagne and wine. Gather everyone after the ceremony for a piece (or plate) of cake(s) and toasts. Have your reception in the garden of your ceremony venue, or even right in the same room. If you opt for this kind of reception, give your guests a heads up on the invitation, "Champagne and cake to follow," so that guests will know there isn't a full meal and they'll probably have to stop for a dirty burger on the way home.

This reception style is great for a couple who may have eloped, but still want to celebrate with family and friends or for a couple who don't want an all-day event. I once attended a wonderful champagne and cake reception that had an after party at a local cocktail lounge so those who wanted to hit the dance floor could. Everyone paid for their drinks; the old people went home. It worked well.

SELF-CATERING VENUES

Finding a wedding reception venue that welcomes outside catering is the dream for many couples as it gives you the freedom to do as you please. If you are lucky enough to secure one of these gems, make sure that early on in the process you acquire all of the necessary info about what you can and can't do on the property. Questions for a self-catering venue:

- Do they have a list of preferred vendors (caterers, hire companies, etc.)?
- What sort of functions have been held in the space?
- Can you see images of past functions and ask for testimonials? (Doing a # or geotag search on Instagram is also helpful)
- Is there a fully functioning kitchen or do you have to bring your own?
- Are there any specific details about the venue that should be passed on to a caterer?
- How much set up time will they allow? This is important as you can construct your time line around this.
- What are the occupational health and safety restrictions (if any)?
- Do you have to take out public liability insurance or will the venue handle that for you?

WORKING WITH CATERERS

The catering market can be competitive and sometimes overwhelming to enter into as a client. For us having quality, memorable food at our wedding was a non-negotiable. We wanted awesome, local produce that our guests would remember. My biggest tip in producing a catering shortlist is to think of the process like choosing where to go for dinner but on a much bigger scale!

Use word of mouth and testimonials. Do they have good reviews? Check sites like Yelp, TripAdvisor and Zagat. Search for images on their social media accounts of events that they have catered before and of course meet with them and sample their fare.

Obviously, consider the type of food that the caterer produces and how that compares to your needs and wants. For example, do they serve vegetarian, vegan or gluten-free options? Are they open to working with you on designing a menu for your wedding or are they strict with their menu choices?

When hiring a self-catering venue, the onus can be on the couple to arrange the rental of catering components such as glasses, crockery, platters, tables, table linen and napkins, chairs, etc. A wedding planner or coordinator can work with the caterer to make this happen, but this will often be at an additional cost to the catering budget. Check with your venue about these details as some will hire these additions in-house, and others will require you to bring your own.

Some caterers may be keen to service new venues, so it's good to connect and see if there might be some negotiation on costs, for example, by sharing photographs of your event with them so they can use them on their website. If caterers are supplying crockery, etc., make a note of replacement fees for broken items and check with the hire company if you are expected to return the crockery and glassware clean or rinsed.

THE CLEANUP

Besides having to remove decorations and gifts, the cleanup of an all-inclusive venue is something you won't have to consider as it will be taken care of. When it comes to self-catering venues, if you are in the situation of having to come back to tidy and are using a wedding planner, try to organize a cleaning team to ensure that the rental deposit is returned in full and you don't have to worry about anything after you leave the venue. One disadvantage of the DIY "run-your-own-wedding" option is that returning the next morning with a mop is rather discouraging. You have a wonderful wedding, say goodbye, and then have to return to vacuum the room, fold chairs, and clean. Not everyone's ideal start to the honeymoon.

Our venue was a private house, which we hired for two nights (Friday and Saturday). It slept sixteen people. On Friday, we invited our nearest and dearest to come to the property to hang out and help us set up the living room, which we transformed into a reception venue. We hired the tables and chairs, which were delivered on Friday morning. We moved all the furniture out of the lounge room and set up the tables, bar area, and ceremony area, which was in the courtyard of the venue. Our caterer was happy to do all of this for us, at a charge. Instead, we invited our lovely family and friends to be helpers and made them a gorgeous meal with lots of wine in exchange.

It was a wonderful experience. We gathered together friends from all of our separate worlds, and they got to know each other and have a laugh before we all got up the next morning to run around like crazy, getting last minute jobs and pre-wedding chores done. It was a massive team effort, and that made it all the more special.

We all created the wedding together, and we got to spend more money in other areas that really counted, like our amazing DJ and photographer. The morning after the wedding, we had a big breakfast fry up and then with the help of our guests, put the house back together again. It's not everyone's cup of tea, but it worked for us at the time.

Would I do it again? Probably not. At least, I would have hired a planner to work out the cleanup logistics instead of us having to do it the next day, which was fine, but in hindsight, we would have happily avoided it and instead had extra time being hungover with our friends.

BOOZE PACKAGES: WHAT IS RIGHT FOR YOU?

Depending on your venue, you may be offered a choice of beverage packages, which range from full-catered, all-inclusive bars to bringing your own booze. When considering alcohol packages, you should start by looking at your guest list and how much you see alcohol playing a part in your day and celebrations – perhaps if you are organizing a dry wedding it might not play a part at all.

- Do you have pregnant guests, older people, non-drinkers, kids attending?
- Do you plan to serve alcohol through the entire celebration?
- Do you want to serve spirits, beer, and wine?
- Will you be creating a signature cocktail?
- Are you keen to serve cocktails and then move on to wine and beer?
- Do you have specific types of alcohol that you wish to serve at your wedding?

Homing in on these details will help you decide the best package for your day and for your budget. Some full-catered hospitality packages and venues will give you a choice of beverage packages.

TIMED BEVERAGE PACKAGES

In these packages, you pay a capped fee per head for a period of alcohol service. This can be an economical option, particularly if you know your guests are solid, first-class drinkers but always consider the math when it comes to the non-drinkers on your guest list. If 20% of your guest list won't drink at all, will the remaining 80% make the package economically viable for you?

AN OPEN BAR

Paying the bill for guests can be successful for smaller functions. You organize ahead of time with the venue a maximum spend limit and if the limit is reached you can decide whether to top it up or move on to a cash bar. Open bars are a good way to control your spending, and you don't receive a nasty surprise by way of an extra bill at the end of the night. Once your limit is reached, you can either add more money or ask guests to purchase alcohol by the glass after your allotted money has run out.

If you do choose to have an open bar, be sure to discuss with the venue what alcohol is available to order and what is off limits (top-shelf spirits, for example). Choosing a mid-range selection of wines, such as Prosecco (Italian sparkling wine) instead of champagne, and restricting the range of spirits and beer for your guests, can keep the costs down. Vodka, rum, gin, and bourbon are solid favorites and very versatile for mixed drinks.

If you do have a set limit on the bar, ideally your wedding coordinator or planner will be the point of contact to sign off and monitor limits on the day, however, if you are self-planning be sure to choose a friend or parent to be the go-to person for the venue to discuss money. You should never have to think about money or credit cards during your celebration.

SIGNATURE COCKTAILS

At our wedding, we prepared a signature cocktail to serve with our grazing table. Schnappily Ever After was a simple cocktail of peach Schnapps, peach nectar, and Prosecco. We served them in little vintage milk bottles that we later resold on eBay. The cocktails looked cute, but they weren't too boozy. It was a good way to ease everyone into the evening without going too hard core with spirits. Plus we served them food, which also helped slow down the potential impending messiness.

Speak with your bartender about cocktail options and consider asking them to start the evening off pouring single shots and not going too heavy on hard liquor. You want your people to have a good time, but not so good that they need a special ride home before dinner.

If your venue is self-catering, or doesn't serve alcohol but will allow you to supply your own, then you are in luck! Wholesale alcohol is great for the budget, and there are always deals aplenty to find. From buying at bigger outlets like Costco to dealing directly with vineyards and suppliers, the opportunity to save money by supplying your own alcohol can be very kind on your budget.

There is a multitude of wholesale liquor clubs and discount companies online who also offer deals on beer and bulk spirits. Cashback sites like my favorite Rakuten.com (sign up via www.thebridechilla.com/cashback to get a special discount!) also offer discounts and cash back when buying alcohol via their websites. When buying liquor wholesale, make a note of the retailer's return policy. If you end up buying too much, some suppliers are open to the return of unopened alcohol. Be sure to keep the original packaging intact and keep your receipts.

BRIDECHILLA STEPS

> **Get creative with your venue options but also think of logistics like power and toilets (glam!).**
> **Ask to see photographs and references from previous events held at the venue for inspiration.**
> **Be prepared. Write a list of questions and requests before inspecting the venue.**
> **Get everything in writing. Do not sign a contract until you are completely satisfied with the details of the agreement.**
> **Do sweat the little things, especially when they might end up costing you a lot of money, such as whether you can bring your own alcohol and food, or if there are extra cleaning fees.**

A Bridechilla is someone who can plan their wedding and get through the stresses that come with it. We have a firm vision of what we want our wedding to be, but know that we don't need to have a meltdown at everything that goes wrong.

Bridechilla Andrea

The Party

Music and entertainment

YOU'VE FOUND THE VENUE, you've thought about what to eat and drink, now it's time to consider the party and the extra elements that you can add to make the event truly memorable. What sort of atmosphere do you want your wedding day to have? Will the reception be filled with dancing and laughter? Hopefully! If so, is there somewhere for this frivolity to occur – room for a dance floor? Is there a place where senior guests can sit around and discuss all the other guests and bitch about second cousin Sue who has remarried for the third time and is bringing great shame upon the family?

When it comes to creating a party atmosphere your guests will contribute to the ambiance, but having a live band or a DJ to get people in the dancing mood can make a difference, compared to just plugging your iPod into house speakers and getting drunk Uncle Joe to yell at everyone, "Get up and DANCE!"

I once attended a wedding that had a three-hour interval between the ceremony and reception. THREE HOURS. I had time to watch *The Godfather Part II*, redo my hair and eat the contents of my mini bar. It was too long and weird to have nowhere to go in between the two events and, to be honest, a bit of a party killer.

By the time we all reconvened, it took a while to regain the energy we had after the wedding ceremony, and by the time the party found its feet, we were three-quarters of the way through the night. The gap between the wedding and reception put a pause on the fun and affected the rest of the celebration.

One solution that wouldn't have cost the couple any extra money would have been to arrange for guests to meet at a bar or venue where we could purchase our own drinks and snacks (and I'm not joking about *The Godfather Part II*. I genuinely watched it back at the hotel because as an out of town guest, I didn't have any chums to hang out with in between the two events and hadn't had long enough after the wedding to turn on the Aleisha charm and find new friends).

It may sound like I am really dissing this wedding, but in truth it was a great day that could have been made even better by ditching the daytime dead zone. If we had been given the opportunity to get to know each other in the hours before letting our hair down, we would have been kicking our shoes off and reaching peak party much earlier in the evening.

THE SOUNDTRACK TO YOUR DAY

Music tells us how to feel. From aspirational car advertisements to the somewhat soulless saxophone music piped into department stores, we are guided by music throughout our day, and the same goes for your wedding music and entertainment. Planning the playlist can often be left as an afterthought when it comes to levels of priority on the ever-expanding wedding to do list.

Sure, you might pick a band or a DJ, perhaps they will email you a playlist template or a song-list for you to peruse. But for many of us, the prospect of sitting long enough to focus and actually go through and process these suggestions and think about the creation of a soundscape is the last thing on our minds months before the big day.

Nevertheless, for many couples, these choices will play a large part in shaping the tempo of your day. Consider the pace of your event and structure entertainment and music around how you want your guests to feel and behave. Guide them with thoughtful and fun music choices throughout the day .

The Bridechilla Podcast guest Andy Kushner, from Andy Kushner Entertainment Design, specializes in planning entertainment and soundscapes for events. In our interview, Andy thoughtfully compared planning your wedding entertainment and music to that of a film soundtrack. Part of the magic of wedding planning, no matter what the budget, is giving yourself permission to inject your personality and creativity through your music and entertainment design, while also finding the sweet spot for your guests to dance, mingle and if you so choose, rock the heck out!

Creating atmosphere isn't just about decoration and visual aesthetics, it's also about setting a tone with lighting and music. Like your wedding invitations – which are the first opportunity to set the tone and vibe for your big day – when guests first enter your ceremony space, it is the first opportunity for you to convey what is coming up and to set the event apart from every other wedding that your people have attended.

Whether you have a friend working an iPod or a string quartet, think about what sort of music you want people to hear while they take their seats. Is it fun and upbeat? Serious and somber? Sassy?

Of course, the venue itself should be considered. You probably aren't playing Drake in a church – although perhaps if it's a "cool" church then ask what they are happy with you playing. One of my recent favorite albums has been the soundtrack from HBO's *Westworld*, which has a bunch of cover versions of modern songs, performed in a ye olde way that I think would really work as wedding background music. It's are the sort of music that makes people ask, "Is that *Black Hole Sun* played on a pianola?"

Be creative. Ditch the traditional processional music and go for a track that is meaningful to you, and by meaningful I don't necessarily mean serious or somber, or classical music if that isn't your thing. If you are choosing to have a light-hearted, funny and warm wedding service then select music that will work with that theme.

Imagine the wedding processional, your walk down the aisle, to the jaunty trombones of the *Curb Your Enthusiasm* theme song. Anyone who recognizes this song couldn't help but smile and laugh at the surprise inclusion. It sets the scene for fun and possibly something a bit cheeky. If your favorite couple music is hard rock or heavy metal and you think that might be a little jarring for your guests, explore reworked or cover versions of their music as homage.

GET YOUR GUESTS DANCING

My favorite wedding moment was dancing hard...kicking off my heels, going barefoot, and trotting gleefully around the dance floor with our family and friends, who were all rocking out in their own individual ways. We had an amazing DJ, Andy McClelland, who really understood our musical tastes. I danced until he pulled the power plug. The evening was full of unadulterated joy. Sure, I probably should have talked to people more, worked the room, but how often do you get to look and feel that good and totally own the dance floor?

That elusive "fun factor" that I think on some level everyone desires for their wedding, is the connection between wedding entertainment and your guests. You want to be able to give your guests every opportunity to shine. If a packed dance floor is what you desire, then you need to create that opportunity for your guests by considering your playlist, where the dance floor is situated, and who is controlling the music.

We've all been to events and weddings that on paper should have the most amazing dancing vibes, but when the music starts, that dance floor is deader than a nightclub at 7 p.m. The DJ tries their best; there's always the lone enthusiastic drunk guest swaying and yelling at the other guests to join them, "Dance! Why aren't you all Dancing!?" It's a real pickle.

So, how do you ensure that the dance floor is filled with booty shaking guests, making shapes and reaching for the lasers? The good news is, you don't need to fly in Elton John or Gaga to make it awesome, you just need to know your market, and what floats your guests' boat music-wise. Think about your guests and your expectations for your party:

- What sort of music will get them up out of their seats and moving?
- Are they old? Young?
- Will they dance at all?
- What mood do you want to create?
- If you have decided on a renaissance recreation wedding, a local punk band might not be that appropriate.
- Do you want live music, or would an iPod or Spotify playlist suffice?

If you are programming your own playlist, think about what sort of music the majority of your guests want to hear. Of course, it is your day, but if you want the audience to get up and dance, playing a Radiohead album (no matter how brilliant it may be) is probably not going to be a dance floor winner. If choosing your own music sounds too stressful, perhaps a DJ would be fitting.

The DJ business is pretty competitive, and portable sound systems have made it a compact affair. One of the benefits of a professional DJ is that it takes the pressure off you. They should have a good idea about what sort of music to play to get people up and what's the right background music for meal service.

Like all wedding vendors and service providers, it pays to shop around and ask friends and family if they have suggestions. There's a lot of trust that comes into play when hiring the right people to help you plan your wedding. Like any other vendor choice, hiring a wedding DJ requires a leap of faith that they will do their job and help you have the best party possible. You want them to do their work without you having to monitor and give feedback on every task, but you also want to feel comfortable enough to share your goals and ask about progress and direction without being hesitant or shy. When it comes to entertainment and music choices, I encourage you to be actively involved, but don't let it take over your life. Some couples are very lax with their music choices, and other couples can be overly obsessed with details including creating long "do not play" lists (songs that the couple or their family don't want to hear on the day). By trusting your DJ or band leader, you are giving them the creative freedom to choose the music that will get your guests moving. Negotiate a start time with the DJ that gives you maximum dancing and entertainment opportunities. Maybe you could preprogram some background music earlier in the evening and have the DJ start later, closer to dancing time? Let them set their gear up before the reception and arrange a time for them to return and get the party started.

LIVE MUSIC

Bands and orchestras can be expensive but real show stoppers. If you know you want a jazz band, instead of a small orchestra, go for a trio or quintet or hire a band for cocktail hour, then switch to an iPod or a hire a DJ for the rest of the reception. Some bands have flexible member numbers, meaning you go big and hire the 8-person version of their crew, or downgrade for a smaller fee.

Make sure when you are booking the band or DJ that you agree on the times that you wish the band to set up their gear and how long each set will go for. If your wedding is on a Friday or Saturday night, book ahead, especially if your wedding is in peak wedding season (spring/summer).

Some popular bands, like reception venues, can be booked out well in advance, so make sure when you find entertainment you like that you pay a security deposit as soon as possible. If you are lost when looking for a band, check out your local entertainment guide. Go along to see a gig and approach the band on the night for prices and availability. Try and avoid booking a band purely by reputation or after watching a couple of YouTube videos. Have a chat with their manager or band leader and ask any questions, especially if you have specific pieces that you would like them to learn and play that might not be on their set list.

Another path to explore when looking for classical musicians is researching whether your local college has a conservatorium of music. This is a great place to find talented, qualified, and often well-priced musicians. Music tutors and department heads can be helpful in recommending emerging ensembles that may be worth taking a look at. However, it's worth bearing in mind that one of the things guests remember most about a wedding is the entertainment. Fantastic live music during a reception or a skilled DJ will delight your guests and keep them talking about your wedding and your dance floor moves for months (at least that's what I tell myself anyway).

DJ ANDREW MCCLELLAND'S BEST DANCE FLOOR FILLER RECOMMENDATIONS

Although these can change from country to country and crowd to crowd here are some songs which are nigh infallible on wedding dance floors. If you know your crowd well, you can get much more creative than this, but the classics remain.

I'M A BELIEVER — THE MONKEES

A cracking tune by an unfairly underrated '60s boy band. Young people know this because of *Shrek*, older people know it because they were there, Neil Diamond fans know it because he wrote it. This can get almost any dance floor going and thematically it's right on point.

CRAZY IN LOVE — BEYONCÉ

A number one hit known by all, this song has nigh on everything; a massive, fat horn section, and banging Motown beat, a cracking dance routine that some in your crowd may know, a big joyous crescendo, and it's a duet by a married couple about being madly in love. You can even find a version without Jay-Z's rap section if you find that distracting. It may not get everyone on the floor, but anyone under 50 or over 12 will go mad for it, and that's enough for a good floor.

YOU MAKE MY DREAMS COME TRUE — HALL AND OATES

What's not to love about this '80s classic? It's got a great regular beat, cracking melody, and everyone at least kind of remembers it enough to dance to it. And who doesn't like the '80s?

CAN'T STOP THE FEELING — JUSTIN TIMBERLAKE

The kids know it because it's from some kid's movie, the millennials know it because it's JT, the oldies may not know it, but it's funky as all get out and has some sweet late disco sounds in it too. Plus the chorus comes back so often that by the end of your first listening you can sing along. So yeah, what's not to like? Nothing. Shake your ass!

VALERIE (VERSION) — AMY WINEHOUSE

Oldies like it because it sounds like an old track, youngies like it because it isn't. This track is often a bit of a surprise for many people as it's not too overplayed, but if you already know it you get to feel vindicated for knowing a slightly alternative banger, and if you don't know it, the hard soul beat will get you dancing anyhow. Pair it with The Supremes version of "You Can't Hurry Love" and you've got an intergenerational smash on your hands.

There are thousands more dance floor killers, of course. American crowds dig a little more hip-hop and R&B, UK crowds like their indie, soul, and rock a bit more, and New Zealanders are charmingly supportive of their local scene. Wherever you go, weddings are about joy and dancing, so throw yourself onto the floor and get a DJ who loves it too.

An often undervalued but affordable addition to your decor plan is lighting. I'm not just talking about disco balls, lasers, and spotlights (although all have their place at a party amirite?!).

Simple uplighting and colorful washes can make a big difference to the mood of a venue. If there is a plain wall that you would like to sass up, see what you can do to it with lights.

Consider planning subtle lighting changes as your event progresses. Research what lighting other events at your venue have used (use Instagram) and ask if you can visit the venue in the evening to see what it looks like in the dark.

Candles are great for ambiance but be sure to check with your venue and find out if they are permitted. If they are a no-go, you can use realistic battery operated candles instead.

BRIDECHILLA STEPS

> **Decide if you want a live band or DJ and shop around. Go to gigs and ask for references.**
> **Confirm any additional costs for hire of gear, transportation, and overtime.**
> **If the party is really going off, will they stay longer?**
> **Use contacts and recommendations.**

When you let down the feeling of obligation that "I have to do this" because it's a wedding, you become a Bridechilla. This amazing community is giving you the freedom to do whatever is important to you and your fiancé. And when we get to do what we want, it's not stressful anymore, so we can plan with fun and chill.

Wedding Photographer Edit Vasadi Denning

Wedding Photography& Videography

PHOTOGRAPHY IS IMPORTANT. Very important. After your wedding is over, the one thing (besides memories) that you can always look at to remember and relive moments from your celebration are your wedding photographs. Images and video will transport you back to the people and special moments that made your celebration. Good photography also captures the feelings and vibes from the day. I can look at photographs from our wedding day and remember the exact moment they were taken. I can feel the warmth and laughter. It's like a magic brain time machine. Our photographer Louisa Bailey was a ninja. I didn't even know she was taking photos at some points and when we received the proofs, we were delighted. She captured moments that we weren't even aware had happened.

At the outset I want to say that if you are looking for bargains in the area of photography, then I am perhaps not going to fulfill your wishes. I can say that good – no, great – photography can be affordable, but I also want to encourage you to see photography as a section of your budget to consider wisely as it is the only area that keeps on delivering, years after your wedding.

WHAT IS GOOD PHOTOGRAPHY?

You might have noticed that I keep referring to good photography. Of course, like anything artistic, what is good and what isn't is completely up to your interpretation. Taste is individual. It is up to you to decide what you value and appreciate when it comes to the skills and output of a photographer.

Photos tell the story of your day. They capture moments that will trigger memories of people and details of an experience that as we know, often passes far too quickly. Finding the right person (with the right skills) to ensure that your memories live on can be challenging, particularly when you may not have decided what sort of photographer, or shall I say, what style of photography that you are looking to achieve.

Wedding photography has evolved from, "line everyone up," to a much more candid experience. Sure, there is still plenty of interest in group shots and family bunches in wedding photography, but most modern photographers promote their abilities to capture intimate, authentic moments, rather than just posed images.

Documentary photography is all about storytelling, following the day as it happens and capturing those moments that make the day what it is. Documentary photography isn't "look at the camera and smile" stuff, it's you chatting, hugging, thinking, doing. They capture real moments. This doesn't mean that a photographer shooting documentary style won't take traditional (or non-traditional) wedding portraits, those beautiful posed couple and family shots, it just means that as the day progresses they cover it all. This is my favorite type of coverage because as a Bridechilla, I believe you are looking for a real and authentic experience. You want to remember all of the little details and moments, not just the posed shots.

Photographers are artists. They are influenced by their surroundings, art, color, and light. When you are considering a photographer, the most solid piece of advice I can give you is to look for consistency in their work. How does their style fit in with the look and feel that you would like to achieve for your wedding? Is their imagery colorful, or moody and dark? If you are having a bright, poppy wedding and your photographer prefers to take stylized B&W shots, then perhaps, although fabulous at what they do, you aren't a match.

WHAT SORT OF WEDDING PHOTOGRAPHY DO YOU WANT?

When you imagine your wedding photographs, what springs to mind? Do you envisage having a photographer with you early in the day, capturing the pre-wedding preparation, or are you more interested in having someone there for longer to photograph the celebration, dancing, and frivolities? This is not a trick question, you can have both! When starting your search for a wedding photographer, I would recommend a few routes:

- Word of mouth. If you are working with a wedding coordinator or planner, ask for their recommendations. Approaching venues for their advice is also an option, especially if you are marrying away from your home base and don't have any contacts in the area.
- Friends and friends of friends. Do you like their wedding photos? Ask them who took them. Obvious, no?

- Geo-searching on Instagram can be fantastic to see which photographers work locally near your event, or you can look at venue tags of other weddings that have been held at the same or similar locations.
- Pinterest location search – for example, searching "city hall photographer San Francisco" – will allow Pinterest to return results that most closely match your query and hopefully find a photographer who has tagged their image with those keywords.
- Local wedding magazines and blogs with featured images and real wedding supplements are also great.
- Check localized vendor listings on wedding planning websites like The Knot and Style Me Pretty. Please note that these listings are mostly paid listings, so they won't include all vendors in that area. I've heard lots of mixed reviews from vendors about listing on these sites, so don't disregard someone just because they don't pay to be a part of them, it is not a reflection on their photography skills or business acumen.

MEETING YOUR PHOTOGRAPHER

As with canvassing for vendors and venues, having a budget in mind will make your photographer search a lot easier. If you have a photographer that doesn't shoot for under $5,000 and your total wedding budget is $7,000, this perhaps isn't going to work for you! Expand your horizons and move on.

When you do find a photographer whose style you like, explore their portfolio and read testimonials. What are your initial impressions? Here are some quick and easy questions to ask prospective photographers:

- Do they have broad experience working with a variety of people?
- How flexible is their style?
- What are the testimonials like?
- Do they have pricing available on their website? If so, do they offer different packages?
- Who owns the copyright of the photos?
- What is their delivery time on final images?
- What is their social media policy?

Think about the level of service that you require. A wedding photographer who provides no pre-wedding planning service and just turns up on the day, shoots and hands over a disk of unedited images provides a very different service to a wedding photographer who individually edits each image. Each scenario will bring a different cost. Read the contract and know your rights. Reprint fees can be nasty and expensive (especially if you aren't expecting them!). If the photographer that you have chosen isn't flexible on this make sure the package includes a number of reprints and be aware that they own your photos.

MAKE A SHOT LIST

As with the celebrant or minister, you need to communicate with your photographer about what shots are necessary. Be perfectly clear about what style of photography you are after. A good wedding photographer will catch those all-important special moments and be an unobtrusive photo ninja while doing it. If you do want posed family shots, groups, and photographs with specific relatives, be sure to communicate that with your photographer and planner.

A friend of ours recently got married, and although she was absolutely delighted with their photography, which was candid and fun, she realized when they received the proofs that she had no shots of just her and her Mom, and the only shot of her grandmother was a lovely candid image, but she wasn't looking at the camera.

If these images are important to you, make a shot list and give it to your planner and photographer so they can schedule the time needed to cover shooting those images.

THINK ABOUT LIGHT

Different light creates different moods in photographs, so speak with your photographer about the time of year you are getting married and the sort of shots that you desire. For example, sunset shots can be spectacular, but you need to time your movements in and around the moment to capture it.

Consider when you are taking your main couple shots. Is it likely to be full sunlight? If the weather is inclement, what are your options for alternative locations (and what is the lighting like there)?

MAKE YOUR OWN ALBUM

If you are serious about saving money, the photographer produced wedding album could be something that you consider doing yourself. They usually cost upwards of $1,000, but there are many DIY publishing websites that offer the same service for under $100. The trade-off is that it requires work and commitment to actually make the album! Coffee table books look pretty and flashy but they will usually take a couple of months to compile, and you don't always get to pick what shots are featured. If you create your own personalized wedding album online, you can add your own captions and include ceremony notes and details.

Some sites will ask you to download the bookmaker software (for free), and others allow you to upload your images and comments directly to their site. Then you can select your photographs, the layout, color, and text. You choose the style, cover, and quality and within weeks you have your very own published book.

AMATEUR AND HOBBY PHOTOGRAPHERS

We all know someone who calls themselves a photographer when, in fact, they might be good at occasionally taking some snappy snaps but they aren't a professional. They don't make a living out of it, they aren't experienced in all light levels and may not even have all of the necessary gear.

Photography can be a big chunk of your budget, but taking a gamble and going with someone cheaper is risky. You can't recreate your wedding day if the photos are bad! The term amateur doesn't have to mean inexperienced, hopeless and unqualified – but sometimes that is the truth! Everyone has to start somewhere, but you don't want your wedding to be an experiment. You want to know that the images being taken will be in focus and capture memories that will live on for years to come.

Of course, there are plenty of members of photography associations that don't take photographs as their full-time job but are just as talented as professional photographers – but to pick out the good guys and gals can be a big job. Again, you have to pick your battles when looking to save money, but photography is something that I would absolutely advise you to pay a professional to do and know that they are going to deliver on your expectations.

VIDEOGRAPHY

Videography is a lot less expensive than it used to be and many photographers work closely with videographers, so ask your photographer if they have recommendations. Videography is a tricky decision for many couples. The first question to help decide whether it is worth the cost is to think about how many times you can realistically anticipate watching your wedding video again (or making friends and relatives sit through it).

There are pros to having a wedding video made: Maybe you want to watch it for things you missed, to relive your vows, or to try and remember the name of your cousin's ex-girlfriend. But is it worth thousands of dollars? That is the average price of a professional videographer. As well as the cost, it can take months and months to get the finished product back to you after editing.

Choose a simple package that doesn't include a lot of special effects or edit-ing. Hire the videographer for the ceremony, and maybe for a part of the recep-tion. The majority of a videographer's fee comes from editing, so another way to save money is to just get the raw footage from them. You can always have it edited further down the track or you can do it yourself – but don't go for this op-tion if you have never edited before. It's harder and more time-consuming than it looks, trust me!

Even if you aren't going for a professional package, make sure that you have a friend or family member with some experience to film the wedding. You can rent or borrow a video camera if you don't already have one or even, dare I say, use a snazzy cell phone.

Personally, I am a little indifferent towards wedding videography. We all carry video cameras in our pockets, and if budget is an issue then I would recommend inviting guests to download an app, with which they can share their photos and videos that they captured on the day. You can either self-edit or hire someone from Fiverr or Upwork to edit the videos into a neat package and add titles and music, if that is something you think you will watch again.

UNPLUGGED WEDDINGS

Being present, being aware of what is said during your wedding ceremony, is something that you hope all of your guests will be able to do. One of the big dis-tracting factors that can take away from your guests' attention span and focus is cell phones. We have become very conditioned to photograph every single mo-ment, coffee, and plate of food because we carry around these awesome cam-eras in our pockets and purses all the time. Unplugged weddings are when you ask your guests not to use their cell phone or to take photographs during the wedding service. This move is becoming more and more popular, and I couldn't be happier. I have no doubt you have spent a bunch of money booking a wed-ding photographer, a professional person who is there to take photographs and capture the day. By asking guests to put the phones down, they will immediately be more present and focused on the time at hand and not think about filters and angles and posting your special moment to Facebook or Instagram immediately after you are married.

There are lots of fun and clear ways that you communicate this decision to your guests including signs and also asking the celebrant, minister or whoever is performing your wedding service to ask your guests to pop away the phones. You can also request that guests do not immediately post images of your wedding day to social media, if that is important to you. This gives you the freedom to choose a photograph to post and share yourself. Some ideas for unplugged signs:

- There's a person here taking pictures. We asked them to come. So please rest your cameras. Our ceremony needs only one.
- Please let our professional photographers be the only paparazzi during our ceremony.
- Oh snap! Thank you for coming. We have but one plea. Please keep our ceremony camera-free. Though our 'I dos' are unplugged, our reception is not. Once we finish our first dance, you're free to take a shot.
- We really want to see your faces. Not your devices. Please put away phones and cameras until after the first dance.
- Welcome to our unplugged ceremony. Please turn off all cell phones, cameras, and any other device and enjoy this special moment with us. Thank you!
- The couple request the joyful sight of your smiles without the distraction of electronic devices or cameras.
- Please keep our ceremony camera-free. We've hired professionals to capture our wedding. So please let us be the first to share pictures as the newly-married couple.

BRIDECHILLA STEPS

- > **Always insist on owning complete copyright of images.**
- > **Decide on the style of photographs and how you want the photography to work prior to the wedding day.**
- > **Create a list of must-have shots.**
- > **Show the photographer examples of the style of poses, etc., you wish to have covered.**
- > **Don't scrimp on photography but do shop around and get value for money.**
- > **Save some money by making your own album.**

A Bridechilla knows her strengths and weaknesses when it comes to wedding planning. She also knows when it all gets overwhelming and asks for help.

Your Crew

Real friends, splinter friends and FYLTHs

IN YE OLDEN TIMES, a large group of bridesmaids provided an opportunity for showing off the family's social status and wealth – the more you had, the higher up the ladder you were. They were also there to confuse evil spirits so they wouldn't know who was getting hitched.

Today, the number of bridesmaids in a wedding party can be dependent on many variables, including the bride asking all twelve of her best friends because she doesn't want to hurt anyone's feelings, the bride fueled by four champagnes over-enthusiastically offering a friend a place on Team Bridesmaid and then regretting it the next day, and one of my favorites, when the number of bridesmaids hinges on how many close friends the groom has so the bridal party doesn't look unbalanced.

I'm going to let you in on a little secret that may help if you are struggling to decide who to select as your bridesmaid. If you're worried about cost and potential drama, or you're not into having a Stepford-style girl crew in matchy-matchy dresses all line up next to you on the day, then ditch the tradition all together.

It's as easy as that.

Ditch the idea and move on with your life.

I know a lot of Bridechillas struggle with this decision as the practice is often considered just something you should do. Hopefully though, by now, you understand that being a Bridechilla is about forging your own path. If that path does not include a gaggle of gals dressed in matching outfits, that's cool.

Many of our modern wedding rituals are based on traditions, superstitions and social oddities. When you break them down, they are fairly naff. Unless you're the Kardashians (and even that's a stretch), you probably aren't focused on the symbolism and social hierarchy of the bridal party and the only evil spirit that may mar your day is tequila. Ditching the concept of bridesmaids doesn't mean that you're letting anyone down; in fact, if you don't have any bridesmaids at all, then it's harder for feelings to be hurt because no one can be left out if no one is chosen. If bridesmaids aren't your bag, if you are struggling with the decision, then consider embracing the traditions and customs that work for you and drop the ones that don't. Create your own traditions, don't work around outdated ones just because everyone else does.

Stressing over bridesmaids and groomsman takes up a lot of time and energy, and I think life is too short for that, especially if deciding between people or dealing with politics is challenging for you. Circumstances change, people change, and relationships change. Just because you were in a friend's wedding eight years ago doesn't mean you have to reciprocate today and boozy promises from yesteryear aren't legally binding.

LET'S STOP BRIDESMAID BASHING

I think bridesmaids have been getting a bum rap recently. When did these close friends go from ladies who turn up to the church on the day in a nice dress (exactly what our mother's bridesmaids would have done) to pre-wedding slave friends – emotional punching bags that organize everything from strippers to destination getaways, people who are expected to go into debt to pay for a dress and talk you off a ledge when the napkins that you ordered are delivered without the lacy imprint? Sure, you aren't that type of bride, you are a Bridechilla, but the evolution of the bridesmaid has been swift and I think rather brutal. Bridesmaids, maids of honor and groomsmen are people who you both can rely on to help you out, plan a super awesome bachelor and bachelorette party (if that's your style) and placate any wedstress.

AVOIDING UNNECESSARY DRAMA 101

My wish for you is a drama-free build up to your wedding day. Dramas usually happen when people don't get what they want, when they don't feel heard or they feel left out. The good thing about families, and in particular siblings, is that they just tell you why they are angry and you can go about fixing the problem – or just yell at each other. Friends can be a trickier proposition.

In a bridal party situation, you are sometimes creating a new group dynamic, throwing people together that perhaps haven't gelled before. I've witnessed some odd behavior from bridesmaids who IRL are mature, nurturing people but for some reason when part of a bridal party, they go off-piste. Whether it's brought on by stress or pressure, questioning where they fit into your life or perhaps they are single or struggling with future choices in their own relationships, bridesmaids that go rogue and don't seem happy to be there, that go out of their way to make the rest of the bridal party feel shit, are often dealing with their own stuff. There are multiple reasons why people act differently than you were expecting them to.

Be kind. Be aware and try to understand their perspective, even if it's unreasonable. Weird and out of the ordinary behavior is often a cry for help, a reaction to them dealing with circumstances in their own lives. Maybe they're single and challenged by your happiness? Perhaps their own relationship isn't as joyous as they project? They might also be worried that your friendship has perhaps evolved in a way they weren't ready for, or maybe they're just having a shit time at work. Who knows, just do your best. Don't feel the need to be Oprah, but do try and channel your best Bridechilla vibes.

Groomsmen can also have these problems, but because they are men, they tend to just hold it in for the next 28 years, then casually at their kid's graduation BBQ, one will say to the other, "Gee Phil, when you picked John over me as your best man, well, that was kind of harsh," and then they shake or man hug and move on.

HOW DO YOU CHOOSE WHICH DRESS IS RIGHT?

When it comes to clothing the bridal party, get ready, it can be a hell of a ride. This is your day and what you want is important, but you should also be aware when dressing your nearest and dearest friends (maidchillas, groomsmen, maid of honor) for your wedding that they aren't Barbie and Ken dolls. They are individual humans with different body shapes, senses of style and their own free will. Not everyone is going to be happy and comfortable with what you may envisage them wearing, and it brings me to ask, why must we dress everyone in the same clothes? Tradition of course. I dare you to break it!

The bridesmaid tradition originated from Roman law, which required ten witnesses at a wedding in order to outsmart evil spirits believed to attend marriage ceremonies (otherwise known as your future mother-in-law! Boom-tish! Sorry). The bridesmaids and ushers dressed in identical clothing to the bride and groom, so that the evil spirits wouldn't know who was getting married. So it has a bit of history. Fine. Whatevs.

I know a lady who chose her bridal party by their body shape and size (only the skinny chicks) and left her best friend, who had just had a baby, off the list because she "didn't suit the dress." It was superficial and it sucked, denting a lifelong friendship all because she thought the photos would look better.

Freedom of choice is a wonderful thing, yet when it comes to style and taste, everyone is different. Yes, your wedding party's attire is a reflection of your personal style and flare, however asking for suggestions and feedback from your crew can make it more of a democratic process and also ensure comfort and happiness for all.

WHO PAYS FOR WHAT?

Good question. Googling this is fun and confusing. It's a fiercely contested grey area and to be annoying I'm going to say it really does depend on where you live. In my home country of Australia, maidchilla dresses are usually funded by the couple, whereas I know many Bridechillas in the USA ask their maidchillas to pay for their own dresses.

Whichever path you are taking, I encourage you to be open and communicative with your bridal party about the expectations of their attire and who is paying for what. Talking about money is never easy, but if you are open and honest about what you would like versus what they can afford (or you can afford), everyone will be on the same page and there will be no need for any animosity or potential weirdness.

Maidchillas might say, "Hey lady, if you want me to wear that taffeta monstrosity that may or may not be a bedspread, which I will NEVER wear again, then you pay for it."

Bridechillas may say, "Hey, I've held your hair while you vomited and I never acknowledge that your fake tan is too dark, give it up and buy the goddamn dress that I want. I'd do it for you."

Having been a maidchilla and a Bridechilla, I will say both parties are right. But it's pretty important to discuss with your bridal party who's paying for what before making any decisions. This includes other wedding events such as bachelorette parties, especially if there are travel expenses and time off work involved.

If the bridal party is paying for the dress/suit, then discuss a budget. Be mindful that financial situations differ and not everyone has $400+ to spend on a cocktail dress and shoes. If it's awkward to talk about this with the group, then discuss it individually.

Don't pressure your friends or make them feel uncomfortable. Yes, you may want everything to look and feel right, but surely your relationship is more important? If it's between them paying their rent or buying your gown, then take that into consideration for the sake of your friendship, and for the sake of them having a roof over their head (and not sleeping on your couch post-wedding).

If you can afford to pay for the bridal party attire, fab, do so, and then you have a little more power of persuasion. If not, perhaps come to a compromise. If you are requesting that they wear the same jewelry, makeup, hairstyles, cufflinks, etc., it's a nice gesture for you to pay for these additional items, or even give the jewelry as a gift for your attendants.

When looking at outfits and combinations for the bridal party, consider different body shapes and sizes. Who will be comfortable in what, and is there a possibility of the attendants being able to wear their dress or suit in the future? It would be wonderful for your friend to enjoy wearing their wedding outfit to other events instead of it just hanging in their wardrobe for the next five years. They might be a lot more obliging paying for the outfit if they think they will be able to wear and enjoy it again.

GO MISMATCHED

The current trend of mismatched maidchillas is awesome. It's an ideal solution to catering to different body shapes and a lovely way to personalize their attire and still stick to a theme or color scheme. You can, for example, select a color/length/designer and let your bridesmaids choose their own dresses. Or, if you are having the dresses made, choose the material and let the bridesmaids select their own style of dress that suits them, maybe a mini, Grecian, halter, strapless, off-the-shoulder, etc. They will be grateful to be able to select a dress cut that they are comfortable in and that flatters their bodies and makes them feel fabulous!

If you are going for bridesmaid dresses that are identical, head on over to the information super highway. There are plenty of websites that offer a wide range of simple formal gowns and dresses in lots of colors and sizes. They also offer swatches so you can purchase the same color dresses in different sizes and cuts. If you are ordering online, allow at least two months for shipping, alterations, and returns if necessary.

I spoke with a Bridechilla recently who said that she had done a massive order from asos.com, choosing a big selection of styles, sizes and colors for her maidchillas. They made a day of it trying on the dresses and deciding together what suited. After the decision was made, they simply sent back all of the unwanted dresses and got a refund. I think this was a lovely idea for the group to bond and sample some dresses without having to leave the house!

Another amazing option is renting your maidchillas' outfits from companies like renttherunway.com. It's extremely affordable, you can use coupon codes to get discounts. Your maidchillas can try on the dresses on before the big day, and again rent multiple dresses to see what suits. They have a huge selection of high-end designers that would be pretty pricey to purchase for the day but can be rented for a song.

For our wedding I wasn't interested in the typical bridesmaid get up. I asked my maidchillas to wear their favorite little black dress, and I found some gorgeous patterned pashminas (that I gave them as a gift) which tied them together without putting them under any additional financial pressure. They loved what they wore because they chose it.

This is the same for the groomsmen's suits, some cuts may flatter and others not. For more casual weddings, groomsmen can wear their own trousers and have matching shirts or ties to bring it all together. Much like renttherunway.com, suit rental has really evolved.

Companies such as generationtux.com offer competitive pricing, free trials and state of the art fittings. They provide quality suits in literally thousands of color combinations so if the groomsmen and groom choose to hire they can have their suit organized in advance. They have some pretty high-tech algorithms that ensure a suit is correctly fitted and also offer free returns and exchanges if the suit isn't right.

This is a great alternative to the wedding party visiting a local suit rental store days before the event, especially if they reside in different places. I love this option, especially if your Groomchilla wants to wear a quality suit but isn't interested in paying potentially thousands of dollars for a tailored suit that he may only wear once every few years.

NEVER WORK WITH CHILDREN OR ANIMALS

Toddlers are cute because they are tiny people. It's fun to dress them up like adults because they're small and don't have the language capacity to resist. Grand wedding plans are created around children, little people who poo their pants and scream for no reason. Think carefully about including little ones in your ceremony because anything can and will happen and when it does it may be uploaded to YouTube and make you rich or at least internet-famous for six minutes.

You're probably better off training a cat to be your ring bearer than your nephew. I've attended a few weddings where an 18-month-old stumbles aimlessly down the aisle like a drunkard, dropping the ring cushion 5 feet before he reaches the groom and cries until everyone says, "Ahhhhhh!" and someone else takes the ring to the groom. Funny, but sometimes awful.

When it comes to dressing tiny people, they sure do look cute in mini tuxedos and flowery dresses, but realistically, the way kids grow they are never going to fit into these clothes again. Shop around, especially online, and be mindful of not purchasing too far in advance as boy do those little people grow fast!

Your bridal party is your A-Team because they love you and you love them, and they want to share the day with you and vice versa. Your wedding day will be amazing because they are there beside you, clinking glasses, dancing like maniacs at the end of the night. Remember that your wedding preparations are really but a short moment in your life and these ladies and gents will be there long after the confetti is swept away. Yes, it's your day, but trust me, with everyone around you having a brilliant time and enjoying themselves it's all the better.

WHAT TO DO WHEN SOMEONE THINKS THEY ARE IN THE BRIDAL PARTY BUT AREN'T

One potentially uncomfortable and sometimes mortifying situation is when a friend presumes they are going to be asked to be a part of your bridal party or wedding team and they aren't. It's a bummer for everyone because this scenario feels a little high school, but there's rarely a day that goes by where I am not asked by a Bridechilla about how to let someone down who thinks that they are in but as Heidi Klum says, "Zay are out."

What's the best way to tell them? Should it be in person? Over the phone? I'm all for honesty. As awkward and occasionally confronting as it can be, in the end, honesty is the easiest and swiftest route. If this person is certain they're going to be asked to be a bridesmaid and they haven't made the team, then an attempt at a one on one is the way to go. If they're long distance pals, then a Skype or phone call is cool. Texts are impersonal and can be misinterpreted in a hot moment. Avoid, avoid, avoid.

HOW HONEST SHOULD YOU BE?

You know this person. How do they react to real honesty, fully taking a trip to truth town? Is it sometimes best to hover around reality, but spice it up a bit to lessen their reaction? I'm not advocating lying, but sometimes cushioning the blow and not making your friend feel shit is a nicer option. If you feel comfortable with saying something like, "We just haven't been as present in each other's lives lately," they might think this too! Sometimes it's easier if they are looking for an explanation to say, "We've decided to keep the bridal party small." (Just be sure not to have eight bridesmaids, or you may look like a dick!) You can also try, "We're feeling the financial pressure, so have cut the numbers of the bridal party," which is difficult for people to react badly to. Whatever you choose, do it early. Don't put it off because the longer this person thinks they're on the team, the harder it is for everyone later. Be mindful of their feelings. Consider what you would want to hear if the roles were reversed. The goal is to minimize drama and maximize the good times. Don't be an A-hole. Be a Bridechilla.

CAN I INVITE THEM TO OTHER WEDDING-RELATED EVENTS?

You want to avoid unintentional *Mean Girls* moments with this choice. The decision of what events you'd like to include them in and what not to invite them to should be made early. The last thing you want them to feel is that they nearly made the team but not quite. Again, this all depends on how cool your friend is with your decision to leave them out of the bridal party. If you are organizing activities that are just with your bridal crew, perhaps you should choose not to include them in the smaller group activities. If there is a larger group involved then go for it.

IS IT OKAY TO OFFER TO GIVE THEM ANOTHER SPECIAL ROLE IN THE WEDDING?

Absolutely! They might be far more suited to the role of an MC or maybe they are fantastic speech makers. I think asking them to be a part of the wedding in some capacity is a nice gesture.

WHAT IF THEY ARE DEVASTATED. HOW DO YOU HOLD YOUR GROUND?

Often people say things in the heat of the moment that is for dramatic effect (watch any episode of the *Real Housewives* for examples). Some people are better at being level-headed and understanding in times of pressure and emotion than others. Hopefully, if you're good enough friends, you can weather these discussions without taking on too many long-term dents to the friendship.

As my grandmother would say, "Let it all wash over you." If awful things are said, then you've probably made the right decision not inviting this person to be a bridesmaid. Grudges and regrets are not worth the energy. Bridechillas take it in their stride, are calm and do what's right for them – without being an A-hole.

BACHELORETTE AND BACHELOR PARTIES

Oh boy. The pre-wedding celebrations are becoming events in themselves, and the expectations of these parties (and trips) are often extravagant and crazy. What started as a symbolic last hurrah, a night of potential debauchery, wearing sparkly veils and drinking until you lose your shoes, has recently become a much bigger affair and, to be honest, I don't dig it.

One night of fun is doable for everyone. You go to a bar or book a venue, have dinner, get sloshed and go to a club or wherever. But now bachelor and bachelorette parties have become beasts of events where people are expected to take time off work and travel to exotic destinations. This is on top of all the money and time that we are asking our people to commit to our actual wedding. Don't get me wrong, I love a holiday. I enjoy drinking cocktails and travel, but I like to choose who I am traveling with, when it's happening, and how much I spend; three points that are seemingly uncontrollable when it comes to these new types of B&B parties.

The bachelorette Grinch I am not, but so often I've heard about the pressure to create these flashy and adventurous experiences. The bridal party feels that this is what the couple wants and expects. Of course, people can decline invitations, but like buying attire it can be hard to say, "I can't afford this," or, "Yes, I will use my precious vacation time and savings to travel to Mexico with 20 people I barely know." FOMO and not wanting to let your friends down can override the sensibility chip that says, "Perhaps skip this one."

One of our close friends was a groomsman in a wedding recently, where he was asked to contribute $800 to a surprise weekend. Two days before they departed, he found out they were going to Dubai, in the Middle East, which was an 8-hour flight away – for three days. He said that it was exciting, but hugely expensive and exhausting to fly that far to go to a water park and drink for two days before turning around and coming home again.

I get the thrill of a group holiday, of going somewhere fun and warm, of wanting to share this experience with your closest friends, but if you are considering asking your friends to come on a trip that may be expensive and will require a passport, then be mindful of how this could be perceived and the pressure placed on people to attend (whether they share that with you or not).

IF YOUR BRIDAL PARTY IS ORGANIZING

Traditionally, organizing the bachelorette and bachelor celebrations is done by your bridal party. Saying that I feel we have evolved past the surprise element and many Bridechillas and Groomchillas are organizing their own celebrations or at least being part of the WhatsApp chats and discussions. If you are leaving the organizing of the day/evening/weekend to a bridesmaid, groomsman or friend let them know what you want. Be clear on exactly the type of party or event you would like and who you would like to attend. Give the organizer a list of friends with their contact details and then leave it in their capable hands.

WHY DO WE GO OUT ON THESE NIGHTS?

- To bond?
- To get mashed?
- To walk around in awful veils and phallic necklaces?
- To have a last crazy, sexual hurrah?

If you answered "a last hurrah", then perhaps rethink the wedding. Otherwise, bachelorette and bachelor parties can be anything from a dinner and drinks with friends to a completely mental *Hangover*-style adventure, with tigers and shaved heads. It's whatever you want it to be and can be a great way for all of your friends from different worlds (work, family, college) to get together and connect before the big day. All eyes will be on you for the evening, so indulge! Revel in the party spirit and remember everyone is there to celebrate with you. If your friend's plans involve dressing you in a silly outfit then go with it, as long as it has a crotch. Your friend just wants the event to be unforgettable (also remember you are autonomous beings so if you don't feel comfortable doing something, speak up).

Enjoy the surprises and don't give in to temptation and probe your friends for details on the event; it will only spoil the plans and the overall effect of what your girlies and guys have in store for you. Don't opt to hold the bachelorette and bachelor celebrations the night before the wedding. This is asking for trouble and potential vomiting. Even if you aren't going hard on the booze and late nights, try and plan recovery time so you aren't stressed by last-minute organizational tasks that may be on your mind. There are plenty of activities that are fun, inexpensive, and a little on the alternative side:

- Organize a bridal-theme scavenger hunt.
- Go to a Soul Cycle class or if you're into the outdoors, do a Tough Mudder or another variety of extreme exercise that gets you muddy and hyped.
- Visit an art gallery followed by a posh boozy lunch.
- Create a delicious bridal brunch.
- Host a dinner party and ask all guests to bring a dish, pick a theme to make it easier.
- Jump aboard a winery tour.
- Create a theme for the day such as chocolate tour a chocolate factory and then go to an ice cream parlor and eat chocolate sundaes followed by chocolate cocktails at a bar.
- If it is racing season, get dressed up and head out for a flutter.
- Host a whodunit murder weekend.

Grandmas, moms and aunts love bridal showers. They usually don't contain too many penis references, and it gives them an opportunity to make cakes and for us to eat them. Don't deny anyone that; cake is good. Although traditional bridal showers might go against the foundations of feminism and can be naff, bridal showers are fab for getting free stuff for the kitchen that you have been avoiding buying or couldn't warrant spending the money on for years.

Unlike bachelorette celebrations where you invite your nearest and dearest friends, bridal showers are a good opportunity to invite the "outer circle," including mother-in-laws, second cousins and annoying relatives. You can make bridal showers whatever you want, they don't have to be tied to the kitchen or patriarchy.

An etiquette guide from the 1920s suggested showers should be "purely spontaneous and informal," with guests arriving unannounced at the bride-to-be's home. This is my worst nightmare. I hate the pop in, they should be banned. I want to know when I should be wearing a bra at least.

Nowadays bridal showers are hosted at home at a specific invited time and a meal or afternoon tea is served. Adding a bit of booze can also make things fun, half a glass of champagne and Aunty Mary will reveal all. A gourmet-theme tasting shower with wine, chocolate or cheese is also a great option. Get the professionals in or do it yourself.

For gifts, pick a theme like glassware or bakeware. If you've always wanted a Kitchen Aid mixer or blender, then this would be the perfect opportunity to suggest it as a gift. Maybe you don't need gifts at all? If so, use this as an opportunity to gather your people and have a nice time or just ditch this event altogether. No rules.

CELLAR PARTIES

If you like wine, then you're about to hit the jackpot. Cellar parties are a great alternative (or addition) to bachelor and bachelorette parties and all of the other pre-wedding celebrations. At the end of the party, your wine cellar will be full. Full, I tell you. It's pretty simple. You invite guests, both male and female, to a party at your home and ask them to bring a bottle of wine. Serve some cheese and snacks, open a couple of bottles and at the end of the party, you have enough wine to last you a year. Another nice idea is to keep the gifted bottle for when the guest visits your home in the future to share with them! It's a nice idea but let's face it, if you're like me, that wine will be gone pronto.

Getting hitched and going through the wedding planning process is a superb time to clean house of people that don't make you feel good, splinter friends, ambiva- lent friends, toxic friends and Friends You Love To Hate (FYLTHs).

This period of your life is an opportune time to reflect on your relationships and what people mean to you and you to them. As adults, it can be hard to assess our relationships and then make changes, even when it could be better for us in the long term. This doesn't have to be a dramatic evaluation, but so much of the details of weddings revolve around the people who are the closest to you and who you want to share this time with.

The guests – bridesmaids, groomsmen, family, friends – are all huge play- ers in your wedding celebrations. Lots of the correspondence I have received from Bridechillas revolves around the feeling of obligation and confusion when it comes to old friendships. Many find themselves clinging on to a relationship that may not necessarily exist anymore. Friendships change and evolve. This is normal.

I know for many couples, wedding planning taps into a struggle with assessing where friends fit into your life. It can challenge who you think is important to you and what they mean to you. It's normal to think, "I promised that she would be a bridesmaid but I haven't seen her in three years, and now I feel incredibly guilty because I would like to ask my new friend to be a bridesmaid instead," or, "I just don't feel as connected with him as I thought I would. I am worried that not hav- ing him be a part of our wedding ceremony will end our friendship."

When I talk about cleaning house I don't mean a mass dumping of friends; it's the opposite. Look at the people that you surround yourself with, ask yourself how they make you feel and what you could do to improve and strengthen those relationships. Are you honest with each other? Are they friends of convenience? Perhaps you hang out and watch Bravo together but would never disclose some- thing deep and personal about yourself or your partner? The word obligation is something I would like you to obliterate from your wedding planning. You shouldn't feel obliged to do anything, let alone have people involved in your wedding that you don't feel comfortable with. If you have to pretend to enjoy their company, or, plain and simple, they don't make you happy, then they shouldn't be at your wedding (and perhaps shouldn't be classified as friends in the first place).

AMBIVALENT FRIENDS

Ambivalent relationships are the sort of relationships that make you feel either neutral or just "blah." You don't love hanging around with that person but it can be challenging cutting ties. It all feels like it is more trouble than it is worth. You persist, but you never grow together.

I'm sure we are all aware of toxic relationships, those relationships that are based upon unhealthy habits such as jealousy, control, objectification and passive aggressive behavior. Genuine friendships are mutually supportive; you should enjoy each other's company and care about each other. Ambivalent friendships can be just as draining as toxic friendships. They might not be as obviously damaging, but having someone in your life like that can be emotionally and mentally draining.

An ambivalent friend is someone who sends you a text message and instead of reading it you immediately think of excuses for how to escape seeing them. One way to define an ambivalent friend is to measure how they see your success. Are they happy when things go right for you? Genuinely happy? Or do they react with an air of passive aggression, or say something that could be taken as positive but always leaves you wondering if they meant it differently? That's not great.

People make weird choices. They bring their own baggage to relationships, and it can sometimes be challenging to figure out why they are behaving the way they are. When I got my first TV job, I had a friend who did not react with encouragement or congratulations, instead they were jealous.

My life didn't change, it was a job, I enjoyed the work, but it didn't make me wealthy, nor did I get any special treatment. I worked damn hard and felt that the reaction of some of my friends to a moment of career success for me was to make me feel bad. It turned from, "Good for Aleisha for finally cracking an audition," to, "Oh, now you're going to be famous and probably ditch us all," which couldn't be further from the truth. Jobs are fleeting. Friendships are forevs...well some.

SPLINTER FRIENDS AND FYLTHS

Perhaps you are part of a bigger friendship group where you have gained "splinter friends," people that you wouldn't choose to see solo, away from the group but have somehow gotten into the habit of saying yes to their invitations.

Do you have friends who you find a bit of a chore to meet up with?

Do you feel like you do more work than them in the relationship?

When you talk about them to your partner or other friends, is it more of a bitch session about all the things that annoy you about them, or do you go on and on about the minutia of their lives, the stupid things they do? Do you enjoy it?

Do you leave their WhatsApp messages unreturned because...well, who can be bothered?

Truth: If you answered yes to those questions, you are either a cast member of one of the "Real Housewives" franchises, speaking about one of your on-air BFFs, or you have yourself a friend you love to hate – a FYLTH. A FYLTH is something that you may be in denial about. Maybe you are someone else's FYLTH, and you don't even know it.

FYLTHs are perhaps old friends you keep in touch with because "you've known them the longest." A FYLTH can be a "job friend" who was an ally but now you've moved on to a new career and barely see them but they still message you for wine catch ups, and you always plan to go but don't. FYLTHs can be people that you like to stay friends with on Facebook because their status updates about eating at fancy restaurants and going on holidays are ridiculous, and you might even sometimes read out their updates to other real friends in a posh accent.

How many people on your guest list, or even in your bridal party, fall into the category above? I'm hoping you answered none, but the truth is I am sure we all still have people in our lives that are hangers-on. Maybe it's just easier to see them occasionally than set them free? For me, real friends, even if we don't see each other each week, are people who you can be yourself around without a filter, people who you share a spark with and who make you feel good about who you are. They are people you look forward to seeing, and it doesn't come with any obligation.

Look at the people that you surround yourself with and who you are inviting to be a part of your wedding day. Ensure that they are providing value to you and you to them. We have such limited time with our friends and family, why waste it hanging around with people that don't make us feel good? There is a simple test to determine whether someone is worthy of your attention or not. Spend some time with them; it doesn't matter what you do. At the end of that time together observe whether you have more or less energy. If you have more energy then you have been nourished; if you have less energy then you have been poisoned.

When it comes down to choosing the key members of your wedding and the people that will be there on the day to love and support you, make sure they are people that energize you, and that will be part of your future and not just your past.

BRIDECHILLA STEPS

> **For attendants, pick people you genuinely like. Forget obligation and guilt.**
> **Be honest about who is paying for what.**
> **Don't let them kill the good vibes. Be honest, problem solve and move on.**
> **If you can, get the group together prior to the wedding.**

> If you don't want strippers and party buses at your pre-wedding celebrations, then speak up.
> If you leave an interaction with a friend feeling consistently bad then it's time to re-evaluate if they are a positive part of your life.
> Avoid drama, try and be the bigger person by being open and honest about how you feel.
> People come and go in our lives. Make sure you surround yourself with people who feel happy for you and your achievements.

A Bridechilla is authentic to herself, she isn't held to unrealistic standards.

Bridechilla Tracy

Sweating for the Wedding

And other body image bullshit

SO MUCH OF THE MEDIA deals with how we look or the perception of how we look and body image. The mainstream wedding media lacks diversity in so many ways. I can bet that if I were to visit my local newsstand right now, 90% of the wedding magazine cover girls would be lean, white women with long hair and perfect teeth. I know those women exist IRL. I've seen them, but I wouldn't say they accurately represent all women who are getting married.

There is certainly a market for lean, white, long haired women in the wedding industry – just visit Instagram, it's swarming with them – but I can't help but get annoyed on behalf of every other woman who doesn't look like that and who rarely sees someone of her color, shape, and sexual preference reflected back in magazines and blogs. There are a lot of excellent publications, both in print and online, that were founded to highlight and promote diversity in the wedding media. I can only hope that their reach continues to grow and this eventually won't have to be a topic of discussion at all.

When Rich and I first got engaged, and I proudly changed my Facebook relationship status, within hours I was being served weight loss advertising in my newsfeed and side bar. Immediately I was being told that I wasn't good enough.

A bride loses weight.

A bride shouldn't be happy with how she looks.

A bride should improve herself.

I know this is merely the result of advertising algorithms and that a lot of people make money trading off these emotions and insecurities, but it totally sucks that our first impression of wedding planning is that you can and should look better. Not to mention most of the advertisements are flogging some dodgy pill or miracle bullshit quick fix that won't work.

For many of us, preparing for our wedding and thinking about being the center of attention can be challenging and anxiety invoking. The thought of being on display, being photographed and being given attention when you might not have a high self-esteem and body confidence can make the experience of dress shopping and the lead up to the wedding for some Bridechillas a really tough experience. Then you log on to Facebook and get all of that shit thrown at you.

In the age of Photoshop and filters, Instagram and tabloids, we're conditioned to believe that part of our self-worth is how we look and that we should strive to look a certain way on our wedding day or we're going to regret it – which to me is ridiculous. We feel pressured to be petite when we go to a wedding boutique because the dresses that the majority of wedding shops bring out are sample dresses (they're size two and 80% of us are not those size people). The experience of purchasing a wedding dress is hindered by this idea that you don't fit the sample shape, that no one else does either, and you have to be pinned into it and you don't get that moment of "Damn! I feel amazing."

Positive body image for me is being able to look in the mirror and, instead of seeing flaws or things to improve, see the good bits. No – the fucking fabulous bits! Changing our perspective from the negative to the positive can be really hard, especially when our whole damn lives we've been fed a bunch of bullshit about ideal bodies and what is beautiful.

I had relatively low body confidence and self-esteem throughout my teens and twenties, and I struggled to allow myself to see the good bits. My self-worth was connected to all of the things about my body that I didn't like. I thought that this was just how most women felt. That we should always be striving for the impossible and that when we couldn't reach those goals, we just gave up. My body image perceptions changed over time and in my mid-thirties, I am more comfortable and proud of my body, and more importantly my health, than I ever was in my twenties.

Having a partner who loves you for you and loving yourself is what matters. Being healthy and mindful of ways that you can stay healthy is what counts. Taking positive steps to look after yourself, whether that be eating more vegetables and drinking less booze or getting off the bus a stop early and moving more are changes and improvements that you can make in the long term, not just in preparation for your wedding day.

SWEATING FOR THE WEDDING

On *The Bridechilla Podcast* recently there was a conversation about the #SweatingForTheWedding Instagram trend. Brides-to-be posting workout selfies and getting in shape for their wedding would use this tag, sometimes wearing a T-shirt and workout gear emblazoned with the slogan.

I thought, great, here are a bunch of chicks getting into exercise. I initially saw it as a positive movement, but the more I delved into it the more I found some of the posts alarming. I explored the hashtag some more and found myself thinking that this whole movement was pretty hard core. Some of the comments were harsh, judgmental, and worrying. They were the complete opposite of what I would expect. Very un-Bridechilla.

I feel that a lot of women participating in this group (if I can call it that) were hitting the exercise hard core, punishing their bodies to the point of near starvation so they could look a certain way on their wedding day. The pressure that they must feel goes beyond motivation to tone up; I saw cheerleading in the comments that were sharing extreme ways to lose weight and encouragement to take seemingly dangerous risks.

I know not everyone who has posted a #SweatingForTheWedding pic is suffering from body dysmorphia, an eating disorder, or exercise addiction, and I am certainly not discouraging being a part of a crew who share their exercise tips and work out together (I actually love that). It's just that when you have this negative drive attached to the results, I feel like it is all in vain.

I am an avid exerciser. I enjoy it. It's good for my brain and my body, but it wasn't always that way for me. I was an exercise self-saboteur. I remember my dad saying when I was in primary school, "Perhaps running isn't your thing." I was chubby, and I didn't have anyone cheering me on, so I took that and made it my own I-can't-run mantra and held onto that into my twenties. I played water polo for eight years. That was hard, but I enjoyed it. The energy you expelled in a game, both physically and mentally, was intense.

Running, in fact any active cardio out of the water, wasn't what I enjoyed. It wasn't until I met Rich and he said, "You can't run? Don't be ridiculous, let's go," that I was challenged and encouraged to shut that "I can't" voice down. I'm not going to say that I am a good runner but after my first run where Rich would encourage me to "just get to the next electricity pole," I felt so empowered that I had beaten that voice. We went out again and again and eventually I was running on my own.

It was around that time I also discovered Beachbody workouts and my exercise goddess, Chalene Johnson. I bought a couple of her programs and did them in our lounge room. They were fun and upbeat and I could work them into my schedule without having to pay gym fees. For me it was awesome. I looked forward to seeing Chalene every other day and I am the first to buy her programs when they come out now.

Since then, I've found a bunch of other workouts that keep me motivated. For me fitness isn't about weight loss, it's about looking after my machine, this body that will hopefully keep on ticking and working for many years to come. I want to live for a long time, and I want to give my body every opportunity to make that happen. I enjoy the way my body looks when I do a weight training program, and I know that in order to achieve those results I have to turn up. It's not Rich telling me to get to the next electricity pole. It's me. If you are keen to find an exercise program that works for you, my best advice is to find a connection with why you're doing it and, hopefully, to develop a long-term ongoing routine that makes you feel good and healthy and vigorous and vibrant because that's what it should be. If you are new to working out, you should focus on something that you enjoy. If you like to dance, go to a class or like I did, buy a Beachbody (or something similar) online membership and do it in your lounge room or garage.

SHUTTING DOWN BODY RELATED OPINIONS

It's not just the media that contribute to body and self-esteem issues, family pressures and expectations for Bridechillas to look a certain way can also chip away at you. Comments about weight loss and hairstyles, "Don't cut your hair," or, "Are you going to use fake tan?" can be difficult to ignore. I am sure that they believe in their heart that they are helping and encouraging you to "be the best you" possible, but it can be pretty hard to overlook the "you should change" message.

A wedding is about sharing your love and commitment. The most important people on the day are you and the person you're standing across from. I find it very strange that one of the messages shared by the media and sometimes family and friends is that we should want to go through some magical transformation to be a different person other than the one that the other person fell in love with. So much of being a Bridechilla is being empowered to be you. To really be you. To own your choices and shut down the white noise of opinions that hinder rather than help. How we feel about ourselves can't be magically transformed by a chapter in a wedding planning survival guide. It has to come from you.

- If getting fit is something you want to do, for you, great! Find an activity that you like doing.
- If visiting wedding boutiques that don't cater to your body shape gets you down, don't go back!
- If you have someone in your life that isn't supportive and makes negative comments or makes you feel like you should strive for unrealistic goals (that don't make you happy) then shut them down by communicating how much their comments are affecting you.

BEING A PREGNANT BRIDECHILLA

Life has an excellent habit of throwing lots of stuff at you at once, and getting hitched when you're pregnant to some women may be totally daunting. I get it. Often you don't plan a wedding around a pregnancy and vice versa, however, I urge you to shake off the outdated stigma of a shotgun wedding and embrace the bump. It's the 21st century. Some people forget that (like old people whose brains are stuck in 1957). This is a shame because when you think about it, a wedding and a baby are both joyous things. New family. New life. Let's get cracking, celebrating them both!

THE DRESS

My guess is 98% of gals wearing white on their wedding day aren't holding on to their V plates, so you can happily ditch any expectations around that old gem. If you want to wear white or cream or ivory etc...do it! My advice to all brides, pregnant or not, is to choose a gown that makes you feel fabulous and is comfortable. Comfort is often treated as the hokey second cousin when it comes to wedding attire and that sucks because a big factor in looking good is feeling good. If you can't breathe, sit down or dance without wincing, if you have to wear three Spanx to suck it all in, then maybe it's not the dress for you. If you're looking for prego dress inspiration, then there is a plethora of celebrity pregnant brides to check out, very few of whom hid the bump. Alicia Keys wore a stunning Grecian-style Vera Wang dress, Lily Allen wore an exquisite lace gown by French designer Delphine Manivet and Drew Barrymore accentuated her bump (in Chanel) with a black satin belt. Whatever dress you choose make sure you have a good chat with your seamstress about how alterable the outfit is, as it can be hard to predict how your body is going to be changing.

SHOES

You don't have to be a grandma, but we go back to the comfort factor. If you want a pair of sassy heels, buy an additional pair of flats (there are so many stunning options out there) to wear when your legs and feet say no.

THE RING

This is one that's often forgotten, but pregnancy can cause swelling in lots of different places, including your fingers! Be mindful of your wedding and engagement ring size. If you have a wedding ring fitted while you are pregnant, it may need resizing later on. Another option is to use a cheaper substitute ring on the day (no one will ever know) and save the real ring for when your fingers return to 'normal'.

THE PARTY

Girl, pace yourself. It's a big day...emotions are heightened, endorphins are flowing, make sure you look after yourself and listen to your body. If you need a rest, have a rest. If you want to dance your ass off, then by all means, shake that booty! Be strategic in your planning...work in ways to sit when you can, schedule in little down time moments and use other people to help you. Yes, you are superwoman – we all are – but you will be surrounded by many helper bees that want to assist you on the day and in the lead up to your wedding. Accept this help. Trust me on this. Drink lots of water, have snacks at the ready and make sure you have easy bathroom access! The best thing about weddings, as we all know, is that you'll be inviting all your nearest and dearest to come and party with you and witness your declaration of commitment and love. What better way to celebrate the new life that you are cooking up than with your family and friends at your wedding!

BRIDECHILLA STEPS

> **If you want to get healthy, do it for you.**
> **Don't go nuts and expect instant results.**
> **Find a program or routine that makes you laugh and sweat and feel proud when you are done.**
> **If you don't enjoy it (even if it is challenging), you are less likely to return.**
> **Find workout buddies.**
> **Think long term. Set fitness goals, not weight goals.**
> **Turn up.**
> **Embrace your changing body.**
> **Pace yourself when it comes to taking on extra tasks.**
> **Accept help.**
> **Enjoy the process and know that stressing about wedding stuff isn't worth the energy.**

not my circus,
not my monkeys

A Bridechilla is someone who can let things go, move away from over-the-top Pinterest dreams, be themselves and own it, seek guidance without shame or fear, drink when necessary, cry when necessary, lose it when necessary and after it's all said and done still enjoy their wedding and wedding planning.

Bridechilla Amanda

Bridechilla Style: Frocking Up

FOR MOST BRIDES THE BRIDAL GOWN/DRESS/SUIT is an essential part of the day. Finding your outfit could take weeks, months or even years. It can be a big decision. Do you want to be a meringue? A bedazzled beauty? An Annie Hall suit or perhaps a perky Betty Draper number? Before you cross the threshold of any bridal store, consider what you want to wear and who, if anyone, you want there to help you decide.

DO YOU NEED TO TAKE A TRIBE DRESS SHOPPING?

Wedding dress shopping is an emotive and fun process (for most of us), but it can also be stressful and overwhelming. Taking along a large posse of your closest friends, neighbors, and third cousins to watch you try on potential dresses while they give their open and honest commentary on each dress seems to have become a thing. Why?! This choice is my worst nightmare. Having interviewed wedding dress salespeople on *The Bridechilla Podcast*, I can confirm that allowing a small tribe of hangers-on to accompany you from store to store may not be the best Bridechilla move. Who goes shopping with seven people and since when did the feedback of those seven people equate to what you want? Although it's lovely that there are people in your life that want to be involved in a significant wedding decision, take a long hard think about what you want and whose opinions you value and want to hear. Trust me, if you take the tribe, you'll hear what the tribe has to say, whether you like it or not.

PRE-SHOP TO FORMULATE A DRESS PLAN

Before hitting the stores with anyone in tow, why not take yourself out for a solo shopping trip? You don't have to try anything on, just take some time to peruse some stores and formulate a dress plan. Then you can make a list of where you may like to return to with your designated helper(s).

Perhaps you have a clear picture of the shape, color and look and feel of your wedding day attire. Or, like the majority of brides, you may have no idea what you are going to wear and can't picture yourself in any of the dresses in bridal magazines. This is totally normal.

I don't know about you, but before my wedding I'd never really had the opportunity to slip into a ball gown – a classy party dress, yes, but chiffon and satin? No. Don't limit yourself to bridal stores, especially if you don't picture yourself in a traditional wedding gown. Department stores and online retailers that stock designer frocks are great to explore and some have their own bridal ranges that are affordable. If a wedding dress isn't your style, then perhaps you might consider a skirt and top combo or a suit or jumpsuit. You can buy a gorgeous Chanel suit (skirt or trousers) for the same price as an average wedding gown, and you could wear it again post-wedding...and boast that you own a Chanel suit!

When choosing an outfit, whether you intend to buy from a bridal shop or not, it is a good idea to visit a boutique where you can try on a number of dresses to find a style that suits you. It's one thing to pick something out of a magazine, it's another to see what it looks and feels like on you. We're all different shapes, heights and sizes, and sometimes the dress we think will look and feel fabulous actually looks like a potato sack or clings in uncomfortable places. You gotta try before you buy and not all styles suit everyone.

I'm going to be brutal here, so get ready. Strapless gowns are not for everyone. I know that every Jane and Jill buys them, but if you've got a larger rack, bingo wings, a tummy, you're short, you're super skinny, the list goes on, they're hard to pull off and, to be honest, they can look (and feel) pretty average.

My point is, you should wear what makes you feel gorgeous and comfortable on your wedding day. It's your day to shine. It shouldn't be about what everyone else wears, or what a magazine says you should wear. On your wedding day, you should feel like a jazzed-up version of you, not a character. You want to look back at photographs and think, "Gee whiz, I looked and felt smashing," not, "Why are my boobs hanging out? Or squashed down? Why did I wear the same dress as everyone else?"

Whatever you choose to wear on your wedding day, you want to make sure that you feel fucking fabulous. I keep saying feel because a big part of looking fabulous is feeling fabulous; owning it and selling it. As a Bridechilla, I know you have personality. Let it show. Whether that means wearing cowgirl boots and colorful jewelry or a dress with a big skirt and pockets, make sure whatever you choose embraces and celebrates who you are!

If you don't dig the shape of your arms as much as your gorgeous curves, find a dress with sleeves, get a pashmina, bolero or a jacket. If you're flat chested, don't feel like you have to use chicken fillet boob cups if they don't make you feel like you. If you have gorgeous porcelain skin, experimenting with a mahogany spray tan may not be the best life choice. I resent the wedding industry's message that your wedding day is the day you will be at your prettiest in your whole darn life. If so, what does that imply? It's all downhill from there? Your prettiness has run its course and you're done? Fuck that.

I felt freaking fabulous on my wedding day, but I've had lots of other outfits and hairstyles (and a few occasions when I've got my liquid eyeliner just right) since then when hot dang I've felt good.

There is so much ridiculous pressure for us to look "perfect" (doesn't exist) and amazing and beautiful that going shopping for THE dress to end all dresses can be completely constricting and bordering on impossible. I can imagine why some Bridechillas end up visiting 27 bridal stores, trying on different variations of the same dress over and over again, never finding that one special dress but continuing to look just in case the next dress is THE ONE.

Becoming dress blind is like finishing Tinder. You've swiped right so many times, there's no one left. You just might have swiped past your dream date or dress, but you were so worked up with finding the perfect one/person (I am still going with this analogy) that you missed it. If you have been in this position may I suggest you do two things:

- Take some time off. Do something else. Stop looking at Pinterest and Instagram and change your brain channel for a few weeks.
- When you do return to dress shopping, try on a couple of dresses that are the complete opposite of what you've been trying on. Go to a department store, try on a jumpsuit, or a Chanel suit or a slinky number if you've only been looking at lace.

Change gears and challenge yourself. Your dress blindness may just be that you haven't had the balls to try on something different that you may really love. You don't need to conform on your wedding day because it's YOUR FUCKING WEDDING DAY. WEAR WHAT YOU WANT.

I HAD A DRESS MELTDOWN

I have a confession. I purchased a traditional strapless dress. It was very pretty. It had a lovely big swooshy skirt, and it had pockets. When I tried it on, I thought,

"This is how you are supposed to look, Aleisha. This is Bride Aleisha." Bride Aleisha* did look pretty, and the dress was very nice, but every time I tried it on, I struggled with it. I kept hitching it up, and even though it was boned and rather sturdy, I felt like it was going to fall off, or that I'd be yanking it up all day. The more I thought about it, the more I worried. When I visualized our wedding day, I couldn't see me in that dress. It was like someone had snuffed me out of my imagination!

We were getting married in the depths of winter, and I was worried about being cold (yes, I am a nanna, but comfort should be considered!). Did I think perhaps the dress was lacking the wow factor? Maybe.

I wanted the dress to look "different," so I thought, let's add a belt!

Fourteen belts later, no go. How about a bolero? A sash? A funky cardigan? A wrap? A sequined throw? Waaaaaaaaaaaaaa.

What if this dress is all wrong and I fell for the bridal industry bullshit about what I am supposed to look like, wearing a strapless gown when that wasn't me at all. Ding ding ding. We have a winner!

A month before our wedding I called my dear friend Julia and said, "I'm embarrassed to say this but the dress isn't right and I wonder if you have a couple of hours to go shopping?" She was at my house within the hour. We went on a fast and furious shopping binge, visiting a big department store and picking every cream and white dress that we could find off the racks. Our venue was a '50s house. It was stylized and chic. I love the *Mad Men* just-getting-married-at-the-registry-office look.

Why, why, why did I buy that big dress that ate me?

With every little vintage style shift dress that I tried on, I realized that the dress I had was all wrong. By three that afternoon, I had chosen a gorgeous cream Marino wool Jersey dress that not only made me feel amazing, but it also covered the bits that I wanted to cover and showed off the bits that I have worked hard for!

I loved it. It was $300, and I couldn't have been happier! So, that's how I came to have two dresses. It's not that I didn't like the original dress, it just wasn't the dress that made me feel like me; the new one did. I donated the original dress to Goodwill. I hope that someone found it and LOVED it, and it made them feel gorgeous and special.

A-LINE

A-line dresses lengthen the whole body without drawing attention to your waistline. A-line wedding dresses are also flattering on petite women. This style is very simple and elegant. The A-line can be slender and narrow or it can be quite wide, requiring a hoop. You do need to bear in mind, however, the larger your hips, the wider the base of the skirt will be. Remember, you want to create an illusion of being tall and slim. If the skirt is too narrow, and your hips too wide, it will simply draw unnecessary attention to that part of your body.

EMPIRE

The Empire is narrowest just below the bust and conceals your waist and hips. Starting the waistline beneath the bust works well for smaller busts, and the long line makes petite brides look taller. For the ultimate romantic style, this one won't let you down. The Empire line with an A-line skirt will also do a marvelous job at concealing wider hips. An Empire line with a column skirt adds height and balances a smaller bust.

BALL GOWN

This style suits all brides as it disguises the body from the waist and hips down. It is flattering when worn with the right style of bodice. These skirts are worn with tulle and/or a hoop underneath. They can also be very heavily gathered or pleated at the waistline. This gives them the poof. This style of skirt can be made entirely of tulle, with no other fabric, which gives a very soft, romantic look. The bottom of each layer of tulle can also be fluted, which gives that curly effect and is really sweet when matched with fluting on the veil. This is a somewhat younger style, but very pretty and classic nonetheless.

SHEATH

This skirt is very classy and elegant; it is simply fitted at the hips and falls straight down to the floor. You can have an attachment that ties around the waist like a wraparound skirt, and this can be your train. This attachment can also be quite puffy, so you have the effect of a princess-style skirt that is straight at the front. This style will only suit the bride that has a healthy curvaceous figure. You do not necessarily need to be slim and petite, but you do need a reasonably flat stomach and backside.

STRAPLESS A-LINE

The traditional version of the wedding gown is a strapless A-line. There are now many variations whereby you can have pleats, shoulder straps and the like. The distinct feature of the princess-style gown is the fitted bodice and waist, which continue on to the A-line skirt. This style is very flattering for larger brides as it is simple and elegant, and this creates the illusion of height. However, to make it work, you need to have some bust. Likewise, going strapless is not the most appropriate option if you are big busted. If you are very petite and slim with little or no bust, it most likely will not be suitable as it emphasizes the fact.

VISITING BRIDAL BOUTIQUES EVEN IF YOU DON'T PLAN ON BUYING

Every Bridechilla should go and try on something truly overpriced and ridiculously froofy just once. It's part of the wedding planning experience. It's also an excellent way to figure out what you don't like, which is often more helpful than knowing what you do like. This way you can eliminate styles and cuts that don't make you hum. When trying on a dress, ask yourself whether its comfortable. You want to look and feel great. You don't want to be hitching it up or constantly worrying it's going to fall down all day.

If you want to dance, don't buy a dress where bending isn't possible! Think about what sort of dress or outfit is most appropriate for your day. A heavily corseted bodice might not work if you intend to sit or eat at your reception. Also, a hooped skirt will probably be awkward at a beach wedding. Bridal boutiques do not expect a sale out of every customer and often welcome multiple visits if you can't decide. Be aware though that some stores will charge you to try on dresses and then remove that charge if you make a purchase from them. Make sure to check this when booking your appointment.

Depending on what and where you plan to purchase, wedding dresses can be hugely expensive. Upon finding THE dress, some Bridechillas quickly disregard budget, lose their heads and end up paying more for a gown that they will wear for only six hours than they would for a small car.

Like any major purchase in life, take your time, shop around and don't be pressured to make decisions quickly. Even if you love the dress, I suggest you go away and think it over. Some (and I say some with caution as most sales assistants are freaking fantastic) bridal stores are good at heavy sales tactics. They prey on the panicked or confused and that sucks. Like in *Pretty Woman*, when Julia Roberts tried to buy a whole wardrobe of clothes from the Rodeo Drive assholes and got knocked back, you will know pretty quickly if a particular bridal boutique is for you or not.

You don't have to be besties with the salespeople, but if the vibe doesn't suit you, or they're too stuffy or pushy, take your business elsewhere. There are so many wonderful independent bridal designers and boutiques out there, spend twenty minutes on Instagram and Etsy and you can fill a year's worth of Saturday appointments. Things that may be said in bridal boutiques that may not be true:

- "Oh, you have six months before your wedding? You'd better make your mind up, or you won't be able to get any dress!"
  Sure, some couture designers do require six or even twelve months to order and make a dress. But there are numerous independent designers that provide shorter manufacturing times. You will not be naked or need to wear a sack on your wedding day
- "You look great."
  Some sales assistants are dead inside and instead of providing helpful feedback, just repeat what you have asked for or just say that every dress is "fabulous" and "to die for." I get that they aren't just going to say, "That looks shit, let's move on," but I know I'd much rather have helpful feedback and to be guided to try on different styles if what I have chosen isn't working as well as I thought it would.
- "That is a stunning organza gown with fishtail pleats; it's just what you asked for."
  Okay, robot.
- "If you come back, this dress might not be available is a month/week/hour."
  This goes against the basic fundamentals of capitalism. They work in a store. They sell things. Unless this is a one-off bespoke gown, it will probably be there tomorrow. If they want to make the sale, they'll find you another one or help you with something similar.

THE 'FANCY' FABRICS FIBS

Traditional wedding dresses come in silk or artificial fibers. Satin, crepe organza, taffeta, and chiffon refer to the way the fiber has been manufactured and woven. Both silk and synthetic fibers can be woven into satin, organza, etc. Silk is expensive and most certainly is used as an up-selling point by salespeople, "Feel the quality!" Many synthetic fabrics look and feel just as nice as silk and are a quarter of the cost. Check the label, and if genuine silk isn't mentioned, assume it is synthetic.

Bridal gown designers and manufacturers deal exclusively with one bridal shop in an area, so if you want to get a good idea of the selection available, visit a variety of stores. Most sales assistants will ask your budget range. This is fine, they want to help you. The one area I would be mindful of is when they chuck in a couple "this is a little over your budget, but I just HAD to show you" options.

It depends on what "a little over your budget means" and how willing you are to stick to it (hopefully very willing!). I don't think this is coercive, they're just sharing other options, but if you have a firm budget then ask the sales assistant to only bring you options that fall within your price range, and therefore you won't be tempted to stretch too far.

BUYING A SAMPLE DRESS OR END OF SEASON DRESS

Wedding gown trends move quickly. You can sometimes save some money by purchasing a dress from last season. Many stores discount to shift older stock. Some stores have sample sale days. Join mailing lists and follow social media for updates, especially if you have your eye on a design that may soon be superseded by new designs.

With the change of seasons, bridal boutiques often sell their sample gowns. Although you may think a second-hand sample dress may not be for you, think again. After dry cleaning, some dresses can be like new. After all, many bridal boutique shop dresses are looked after extremely well; they are maintained and cared for because they are what make the sale.

The dresses are usually sample sizes (and sometimes rather random sizes). As always, exercise caution and inspect the dress thoroughly before purchasing. If beading is missing, ask if the store can help you replace them. Check for makeup stains and try the dress on to make sure it is true to size. Remember it's only a bargain if you don't have to spend hundreds of dollars repairing and resizing it. Be aware that all sales will most likely be final with these types of purchases.

BUYING A DRESS ONLINE

If buying a dress in a boutique doesn't interest you, or the variety just isn't there, you may find your outfit online. Sometimes online sellers have lower pricing due to the high volume of sales they are able to achieve and lower overheads from not having a physical store. I'd advise using the same caution in choosing an online company to spend your money with as you would with selecting a bridal shop. If they don't seem right, if their customer service isn't great, if they don't respond to your emails, then don't do business with them.

Factor into the cost any import or duty taxes that may be added to items. This can be up to 20% in some countries and states. Does the supplier have refund, exchange and return options available? Ask questions to ensure that they will take the gown back if it arrives with a flaw and replace it at no cost to you. Have a tailor take your measurements and if in doubt order a size up, as it is a lot easier to take a dress in than come up with creative ways to make it bigger. Bridal stores (in nearly all cases) will not accept exchanges. The gowns are ordered just for you from the manufacturer. If you place a deposit at a shop, it is non-refundable. It is best to be sure of your gown, price and additional details before placing a deposit.

BUYING A PRE-LOVED WEDDING GOWN

Most wedding dresses are worn for about eight hours. They're basically new. If you have your eye on an expensive designer gown that is perhaps out of your Bridechilla budget, consider searching for a pre-loved wedding gown on the many websites that list them for sale. One of the most popular among members of the Bridechilla Community is stillwhite.com. As in any transaction, ask a lot of questions, particularly about alterations and sizing. Also, if the pictures aren't clear, ask to see more. If you can meet the seller to try on the dress, even better.

LESS IS MORE

The simpler the wedding gown, the less expensive it is going to be. If you leave off the beading or embroidery, or simply switch the fabric of the gown, you may save some money. Traditionally, wedding dresses have not always been white. The popularity of the white and ivory wedding dress can be traced back to 1840 with the marriage of Queen Victoria to Albert of Saxe-Coburg. The Queen chose to wear a white gown for the event, and the official wedding portrait photograph was widely published, and many brides opted for a similar dress in honor of that choice. The tradition continues today.

Wedding dresses vary across the globe. Many wedding dresses in China are colored red, the traditional color of good luck. For brides in the northern parts of India, the traditional color of women's wedding garments is also red, a color symbolizing auspiciousness. The color green is also commonly used, signifying fertility. Lots of designers are opting to add color to their gowns, with patterns, dip-dying, and ombré becoming very popular. What was once risqué is a lot more mainstream and I for one am happy we are easing away from the white and ivory strapless gowns and instead embracing a bit of personality and a splash of color in our wedding attire.

CONSIDER GOING VINTAGE

Do you like the 1950s look? Then perhaps vintage is worth considering. Vintage dresses (new and genuine) are massive with brides, especially with the classic

'50s look of wider skirts and smaller accentuated waists. They're very flattering, chic, feminine and fabulous, accentuating an hourglass figure. Not only can you score an original and classic designer gem, but you can also guarantee that you won't see other brides swanning around in your dress. If you don't want to buy online, hit vintage bazaars, fairs, and second-hand stores.

There are thousands of specialty vintage dress vendors online. The disadvantage of buying vintage without trying on first is sizing. Sizes have changed, so be sure to ask for exact measurements. If you are considering buying genuine vintage consider the following:

- Look for general wear and tear.
- Ask where and how the dress has been stored.
- Are there visible mildew marks or stains? Moth holes?
- Has the dress been dry-cleaned? (This could actually be bad if the dress is really old, as some were not made for such a process).
- Is the color exactly like the photograph (you would be surprised how different some of these dresses look compared to the photographs).
- Wearing vintage is pretty special, and the quality of formal dresses was usually of a very high standard. You can also buy "new" vintage. Get the look without the age! There are many companies that have excellent ranges of vintage-look dresses at very affordable prices.

REPLICA DRESSES

This is a risk. I'm going to be honest – a lot of replica dresses are substandard and shit. If you have your eye on an ultra-expensive designer dress and cannot warrant paying the price, you may consider a "designer inspired dress" or a replica or a rip-off, but it's risky, and I believe a little morally troubling.

There are thousands of companies out there that will replicate a gown from a photograph or sample for very little money. I'm talking $200-$500. I'm sure you may have seen some of the heartbreaking/amusing posts online about the outcomes of these little adventures.

I am not guilt-tripping or preaching here, but looking at some of the prices of these gowns, I believe we should assume that most of these dresses are made in sweatshop factories. Maybe not by kiddies, but probably by people that should be paid more. And to be honest, even some authentic full prices dresses are made in these factories.

You should ask questions about what you buy and where it comes from. If you only pay $199 for a replica of a dress that sells for $5,000, then surely we should ask who is making the cheaper dress and what are they making it out of?

Also, replicating designs is against copyright laws and counterfeit goods are illegal and can be impounded by customs, so be warned. Most gowns that are ordered through these companies are produced and shipped from China or Eastern Europe; the online "shop front" generally trades from the USA. Like my dad says, "If it sounds too good to be true, then it probably is."

QUESTIONS TO ASK WHEN YOU'VE FOUND THE DRESS (OR OUTFIT)

- Do they offer a discount for cash payments?
- What is the final price and what does the price include? Are there extra taxes?
- Does the price include alterations and fittings?

Be sure, like all other wedding transactions, that you get a receipt and all of the above information in writing.

UNDERWEAR

I always laugh when I see companies marketing sexy underwear or, to say it très elegantly, lingerie to wear under your wedding dress. Most of the time you are just trying to keep everything in place, using elastic, tape and a carefully choreographed pulley system. Sure, we want to feel sexy. But a lot of the time, realistically, it is a pair of Spanx and a good underwire bra.

Depending on your dress or style of outfit, you may be wise to invest in some specialty underwear which you should have ready to take along to your dress alteration appointments. Whatever you choose to wear, make sure you can breathe, pee, and feel all of your extremities while wearing them (when I say pee, I mean be able to remove them to pee, this is not an adult diaper situation).

SHOES GLORIOUS SHOES

Are you intending to make your shoes a feature of your outfit? Or are they hidden between layers and layers of organza? Are the shoes a showpiece (if your dress sits above the calf then yes perhaps they are), or are you the only person that will ever touch/see them?

Shoes are an area where I think you can justify spending a bit more money, particularly if you think that you'll wear them again. I am the first person to call if you need to convince someone that shoes are an investment. Colorful wedding shoes are quite the trend, bright gorgeous statement pieces that can change a sedate wedding outfit into something truly sassy. If you're going safe with your dress, get some fabulous Wizard of Oz-style heels.

Match the shoes to your day. If you are having a casual event, like a beach ceremony on the sand, then ditch the stilettos as they are both impractical and you'll probably end up crawling down the aisle. Ballet flats, fancy sandals, sneakers or barefoot are easier possibilities. You can wear heels later at the reception if it's on flat ground.

If you have your eye on a pair of uber designer shoes, Google the hell out of them. Discount shoe websites are everywhere but make sure you check the company's return policy. Also, be wary of replicas and rip-offs. Black Friday and post-Christmas/holiday sales are a great time to score a bargain pair of open-toed shoes, especially during the winter. When you do buy your shoes, make sure you wear them in to avoid uncomfortable blisters and pack some Band-Aids on the day of your wedding just in case.

BRIDECHILLA HAIR AND MAKEUP

When you stride, drift or walk down the aisle, your partner is going to want to see the real you, not some freaky, painted, over-tanned doll version of you. It surprises me as to how some people completely transform themselves for their wedding day so that they don't end up looking like themselves.

Jazz it up a bit, yes, but turning yourself into a Vegas showgirl with hair extensions, falsies (boobs and eyelashes), and a thick spray tan, if that's not your usual look, is a little weird.

We go back to the idea that we are supposed to look a certain way, that all brides should have long hair or wear a lot of makeup. If you aren't a big wearer of makeup, then you shouldn't feel pressured to suddenly embrace heavier makeup for your wedding day.

You want to feel fabulous, and when it comes to hair and makeup a big part is finding a look that does just that. If you don't usually wear a lot of makeup, don't wear a lot on your wedding day. You aren't playing a character; it's not Halloween or a dress up party, it's your wedding.

A natural face, with beautiful dewy skin and light blush, can look very pretty. A lot of wedding makeup artists specialize in creating this look which evens out your complexion without requiring heavy foundation and eye makeup.

Working in TV, I often had my hair and makeup done by professional artists. When it's done right, I feel good; I'm confident that I still look like me, but more even skin-toned and with thicker lashes. Too much makeup and I look like a cakey, old bag. I can say that because it's me. You don't want to look like a cakey, old, bloated bag (or if you need a direct visual reference, any Real Housewives of New Jersey).

When working with makeup artists, collect inspiration on Pinterest and Instagram to share with them. Think about color tones you like. Are there parts that you would like to accentuate? For example, I like eyeliner on my top lid, but I think under eye eyeliner makes me look like a junkie. It's a no-go for me.

It is not offensive to makeup artists to provide them with information like that. Having a makeup trial is a way to ensure that you get to work with each other and try a few different looks before your wedding day. I'd highly recommend you consider this, especially if you aren't sure about the look that you would like to achieve, or if you aren't a regular makeup wearing person.

Don't do what I do at the hairdresser and say that you love it when you don't and then go home and punch a wall or cry. Speak up. Be clear about what you would like to change and ask them to do it on you, to make sure you are both on the same page. Be sure to photograph the look at the end of the session, so you have a guide for the day of your wedding.

DIY MAKEUP AND HAIR

The most budget-friendly option when it comes to hair and makeup is doing it yourself. Some people are very comfortable in doing their own hair and makeup. Kate Middleton did her own makeup for her wedding day, and hey, she was marrying a prince. However, I am certain she had someone on hand to check it all and make sure she was "show ready."

Be mindful, if you are considering going down this route, to practice a lot and think about timing. I know when I have a deadline, and I have to curl my hair, my luck is one side works and the other doesn't or God forbid I attempt a fucking cat's eye. I end up looking like I have some form of facial palsy. Of course, when there is no time limit, my hair is high and eyes are even, so, even if you are very confident, give yourself ample time.

BUYING MAKEUP

If you are choosing to DIY your makeup on your wedding day, I would suggest sticking with brands of cosmetics that you have used before. Approach their makeup advisors at a department store and ask for advice about what products they would suggest you use and try. By using a brand that your skin is familiar with, you are less likely to have any reactions to the products and more likely to use again after the wedding. Also, brands like Mac will do a complimentary makeup session when you buy the product, so if you are looking for help to achieve a certain look, turn to a professional!

USE YOUR CONTACTS

Most hairdressing salons have connections to makeup artists, either on staff or that they would recommend. Talk to them about who they work with regularly and trust.

HAIR

Your wedding hairstyle is something that can transform and add to your look. Lately, we seem to have transitioned to more relaxed styles – braids and loose curls, natural down looks without too much fuss. Of course, the loose curls don't just happen, plenty of work goes into even seemingly simple looks. But there seem to be fewer extravagant updos and more casual styling in recent times.

To make sure you get the look that you want on the day, most hairdressers, like makeup artists, recommend a hair trial. Some hairdressers will do it for free; others include the cost of the trial in their wedding day package. Be sure to confirm this before the appointment. If you are going to wear a veil, hair-clip or netting, take them to your trial. On your wedding day, wear a zip-up top (or something you can get over your hair and makeup after it is finished).

If you have your hair colored before your wedding or plan to use color matched clip-in weaves, make sure you leave time for the color to settle. Try and book an appointment for 3-10 days before your wedding and make sure you have patch tests done on your skin if you are using a new color brand to avoid any outbreaks of allergic reactions before your wedding.

CLIP IT IN

As someone with rather fine hair, I am a big fan of a clip-in weave. This is obviously mislabeled because the beauty of clip-in hair (especially hair that has been color matched) is that no one knows you are wearing it. It's great for making your hair look thicker, adding an ombré look if you don't want to bleach your own hair or giving some extra length when you've been growing your hair for five years, and it's only grown an inch.

Buy hair from reputable suppliers. If you want real human hair, I would suggest purchasing from a hairdresser directly. They can fit and cut the weave so it blends with your hair and you can clip it in post-wedding, too.

> There will always be another dress. Don't be compelled to make a decision on the spot.
> Be like Fonzie, act cool.
> For many brides, a process of elimination is your best bet. Try on a range of dresses, even those you don't think will suit you.
> Don't be afraid of secondhand and pre-loved gowns.
> Pick a dress that you love, that makes you feel fabulous. Forget trends and what looks good on waifs.
> If you are using a makeup artist, have a trial.
> Collect clippings and examples of hair and makeup you wish to try.
> Always look like YOU.
> Don't go overboard.
> Steady on the spray tan.
> If you are doing your own hair and makeup – practice, practice, practice!

* I know in the intro I promised to never write in third person again, but I just couldn't help myself. Soz.

For me, Bridechilla was that "Aha!" moment I so, so needed.
FINALLY! A place I belonged!
Yes, we want it to be memorable, but we also want it to be "us" and you know what represents us?
Throwing all the unnecessary stress into the fuck it bucket, grabbing a drink, and chilling the fuck out.
So, that's what we're planning to do during our wedding weekend.

Bridechilla Casie

Invitations, Save the Dates & RSVPs

YOUR WEDDING INVITATIONS AND STATIONERY (including save the date cards) set the stage for your whole event. They are the guests' first impression of your wedding and they set up their expectations of the event. Ultimately though, the purpose of a wedding invitation is to convey information.

- Who is invited
- What they are invited to
- When they are required to be there
- What else they need to do and bring

The look of the invitation, the aesthetics, is where you can really convey the tone and overall vibe of your wedding. It's important that the information you put on the invitation is easy to interpret and understand, and includes necessary information such as addresses and, if the destination is hard to find, directions.

DESIGNING YOUR INVITATIONS

The look of your wedding stationery should connect with your wedding theme or colors or at least have some synergy with the sort of party that you intend to plan. It's a time to get creative and have fun with how you want to convey all of the important information and the tone of your event. Think about the style and wording, and consider what you want your guests to think or feel when they receive it.

Delegating the design of your wedding stationery to an expert is easy. There are many talented independent designers who will do custom designs. Hiring a graphic designer from websites such as 99designs.com, upwork.com, fiverr.com and Etsy to design your wedding stationery can be a wise move, particularly if you are time poor or perhaps not that confident with your Photoshop skills.

It's exciting to work with a designer who gets what you want and whose professional eye and creativity can add to your ideas and bring them to life. Using a professional also comes in handy when you are ready to print your designs – they will be able to help you with bleed and color settings that all professional printers, even the cheaper online ones, require. If you do commission a graphic designer to work with you on your wedding stationery, get a quote for them to do all of your design work, which could include menus, save the date cards, thank you cards, printable signage, and seating charts. If you make that connection early on and you work well together, it's great to have someone on your team who can whip up some amazing work and take that task away from you.

DESIGN AND PRINT YOUR OWN

Designing a wedding invitation might be something that you're really looking forward to. Maybe you are very capable of using Photoshop or perhaps you are into canva.com, an awesome design website that is so easy to use my dad could do it. Font websites like dafont.com and abstractfonts.com are a great place to source free fonts that can help you create a customized look with all of your wedding stationery from place cards to coasters, menus, or thank-you notes.

Before committing to a DIY project to save money, consider the time and effort that is going to go into this project and the cost of the tools to make it happen. I am the first to admit that I get quickly carried away with crafty missions that are going to save me both time and money. I'm pretty handy but even still, 95% of my projects come in over budget, and I am left with tools that live in the bottom drawer of the kitchen just begging to be used.

Is it worth spending every night for three weeks cutting and gluing and getting angry at staples to save $50? Your time is valuable, particularly in the months leading up to your wedding. Wouldn't you rather relax and have a wine instead of breaking down over folding paper? I'm all up for DIY, just know what you are in for before buying all the gear.

If you would still like a personalized experience but can't necessarily afford a graphic designer, or if you want to go it alone, I suggest you visit etsy.com and look at all the diverse options that are available to download and edit, or to pay a little extra money and have the Etsy seller add your personal details to their design. After your purchase and edit, you can then simply take the printable file to an online printing company such as vistaprint.com and order your invitations and stationery to be printed. Often packages are available to save you lots of money if you order your save the date, wedding invitations and thank you cards using similar designs and patterns. By doing this, you have everything ready to go, and also you avoid forgetting about writing your thank you cards because you already have them! If you are ordering online and using services like vistaprint.com, make sure you Google "Vistaprint plus coupon" on a weekly basis as they often have 40–50% off sales, especially if you are regularly visiting their site and they are using their cookies to capture your information.

Remember, the fancier and more detail heavy the invitations are, with jackets, bows, buttons and embellishments, the more expensive they get. As well as the invitation, some couples like to include additional cards such as accommodation, hotel information, and specifics about other events that may be taking place during their wedding celebrations.

Including a prompt to RSVP with your invitation is important, whether you ask your guests to email or call you or include a return card (such as a postcard). You can choose to pre-stamp the RSVP so that all guests have to do is pop it in the mail. The easier you make it for them, the more likely that they will return it and thus save you time having to contact people later, which can be a total drag.

Be mindful of the print size of your invitation and the postage costs associated with that size and weight. It's great saving money by printing and designing your own invitations, but if they're heavy and bulky, you may end up spending just as much money sending them to your guests. For a postage estimate, take a complete wedding invitation to the post office for a weigh in. Include response cards, registry cards, maps, and any other inserts you plan to send to your guests. Local and overseas postage costs vary depending on the thickness of the wedding invitation as well as its weight and size. Square envelopes will cost more to post than regular rectangle-shaped envelopes. Again, you don't want to spend $5.00 mailing the invites because that's an extra $600 if you have 120 guests.

GO PAPERLESS

Another great wedding invitation alternative is to use Paperless Post, a digital invitation service with beautiful designs. You are able to send the invitations digitally and then print a couple of copies if you want to send them to people like your grandparents who may not have access to emails.

CONSIDER CREATING A WEDDING PLANNING WEBSITE

Perhaps you are considering making a wedding website, something that is becoming more and more popular with the Bridechilla Community. It is an avenue that I would recommend if you are looking to save money on paper and postage. A website also lets you add extra information that might not necessarily be easily inserted in an invitation but is something that you would like to convey to your guests.

There are lots of drag and drop, easy to use wedding website creators that will keep track of RSVPs, let you add links to things like gift registries, Google Maps, and accommodation websites, as well as store details about extended parties and other events that may surround your wedding celebrations. I recommend zola. com as a good place to start. Use the codeword BRIDECHILLA for exclusive access to seasonal bonuses!

ENGRAVING

Engraving is the most traditional form of wedding invitation printing, and one of the most expensive. The text is etched onto a copper plate, which is then coated with ink and wiped clean, leaving the ink only in the indentations.

Soft, high-quality paper is pressed hard against the plate, causing it to deform into the etchings. You can tell true engraving by the "bruise" or dent on the back of the paper.

THERMOGRAPHY

Thermography was developed as a less expensive alternative to engraving. The printer uses ink and a powder resin combined with heat to reproduce the raised lettering effect of engraving. The text has a shiny finish and is often said to be not as sharp as engraving.

LETTERPRESS

This old technique has had a massive revival of late. A letterpress printer presses inked letters (or patterns) into a piece of paper, forming an indented surface. By repeating the process, you can create images with more than one color.

EMBOSSING OR BLIND EMBOSSING

Most often used for small insignias and monograms, this process creates a raised impression on paper by running the paper through two metal sheets. When no ink is used, it is called "blind" embossing.

OFFSET PRINTING

Most modern printing is offset printing, also known as lithography. From magazines to postcards, this flat style of printing is a familiar one, and appropriate for an informal wedding invitation. Traditionally, an inked image is transferred from an inked plate to a rubber "blanket," which then passes over the paper.

WHEN TO SEND WEDDING INVITATIONS AND SAVE THE DATE CARDS

Etiquette crazies love this topic. Personally, I think when you send out the invitations has a lot to do with where and when the wedding is to take place. The more you are asking of your guests, the more heads up you need to give them. If you are expecting guests to travel to your wedding, whether it's interstate or overseas, you'll need to give them a bit of notice (and detailed information) so that they can take time off work and plan travel and accommodation. So for a destination wedding, particularly an international event, I would suggest giving them six to eight months' notice before the wedding.

Save the date cards are usually sent out six to twelve months in advance of invitations and allow your guests to know the time and date of your upcoming wedding, so they can book travel and accommodation.

Warning: You can't take back a save the date. Make sure that you finalize the guest list prior to sending, because once they're out there – unless you have a colossal issue or falling out – you're obliged to send them an invitation. Standard wedding invitations are sent out eight to twelve weeks before the wedding, with an RSVP date around four weeks before the event.

If you have a sneaky reserve guest list, people on the B list that you want to try to invite if some guests can't make it, factor that into your timing. If you have a reserve list, it might be a good idea to send your invitations out around three months before the wedding. This will give any guests that can't come time to reply, and for you to issue a new wedding invite to your reserve list without them feeling like they were a last-minute choice.

WEDDING INVITATION WORDING

The wording of your invitation should match your party. Using stuffy formal language like "The honor of your presence" or anything with the word "cordially" is very traditional and I think a little odd to include in a modern wedding invitation. If you speak like that in real life, then go for it. If you are royalty, right on, but if you are a regular gorgeous couple, you don't have to use such formalities. Announce your plans for the future with a wedding invitation that captures the joy you feel and the tone of the event. Typically, the wedding invitation will include the following details:

- Names of the couple getting married (that's you!)
- Name/s of the guest/s
- Location
- Full date and year
- Time of the ceremony
- Reception information
- Dress code
- RSVP information
- Contact details

There are some schools of thought that are pretty traditional. They suggest you need to include both parents' names at the beginning of the invitation, especially if the parents are paying for and/or formally hosting the event. Although, in the end, this decision is totally up to you. Keeping your message short will also make it more powerful and will likely have the best effect on its intended recipients:

Katy + Jack are getting married!
Please join us to celebrate their union
Date | time | place

Please join us at the celebration of the marriage of
Katy + Jack
Date | time | place

The honor of your presence is requested at the marriage of
Katherine Elizabeth
And
Jackson Tyler
Date | place | time

Join us for the wedding of
Katy + Jack
Date | time | place

THANK YOU CARDS

Remember to order thank you notes. This can be the most overlooked task in the wedding, but it's essential. It shares your appreciation and love. Often, this is the last thing you feel like doing after the wedding, so make sure you set yourself up for success by pre-ordering cards. Keep your information, such as guest list and gift registry responses, up to date so you know who attended your wedding and what item they gifted you.

When writing a thank you card, the basic formula is to express gratitude, be specific about the gift, and thank them for attending or for thinking of you if they could not attend. Perhaps tell the giver how you will use the gift. For example, "We used the blender for post-wedding margaritas. Can't wait to make some for you when you're next in town."

If the gift is cash or a registry contribution, thank them for their generosity without mentioning a specific amount. Perhaps they purchased an experience for you on your honeymoon or a new item for your home. Including a photo of you using the item during the experience is also a nice touch.

BONUS PLUS ONES

One fun challenge that often can be frustrating and annoying to deal with is rude guests who add their own plus ones to their RSVP cards. I understand that in different cultural backgrounds and family situations this can occur, but, for many of us facing tight budget and venue space, someone deciding that they going to bring a guest to your wedding is really inappropriate. This makes me angry beyond belief. In no way is this okay, it's guest list violation.

I'm a believer that a polite challenge is one of the only ways to deal with this situation, particularly if the person they've added to your invitation is not someone that you would like to attend. Explain that you don't have the capacity or budget to include the extra guests.

It can be embarrassing and sometimes quite hard to confront people and call them out for the lack of etiquette and manners, but often, especially if the person they have added to the invitation is not someone you would have invited in the first place, it's better to challenge it now and get it sorted rather than it becoming a real issue. Be strong.

WAITING FOR RSVPS

RSVPs are a contentious issue. Waiting for those little cards to be sent back can sometimes feel like time has stopped. Why aren't people replying quickly? Do they not want to come to your amazing wedding? When do you start sending bitchy texts to people asking them to hurry up and respond?

Let's get down to basics. The term RSVP comes from the French phrase "Répondez, s'il vous plait," which in English is "please reply." Pretty direct and clear, thanks France. The person sending the invitation (you), sends an invitation and then your guests either accept or decline the invitation. Etiquette rules followed in most Western weddings require that if you receive a formal, written invitation, you should reply promptly. As well as being just plain polite, guests promptly replying to RSVPs helps couples (and wedding planners) shape the day in terms of both scheduling and budget. Without RSVPs, it's a guessing game as to who is going to show on the day and how many people you need to cater for.

Most venues and caterers will require a cut-off date for guest numbers. Sometimes there is some flexibility, but more often than not it will be a few weeks prior to the wedding. Once the numbers are locked in, that is the figure that you pay. If you make a guess about who is coming, or if someone doesn't show, then you still pay for them.

It can be frustrating waiting for the return of RSVPs. It can feel a little rude. You've taken the time to invite them to this big special event, and they couldn't be bothered to return a little card!? What gives? Well, life gives. I am guilty of a late RSVP. Not on purpose, I had every intention of replying on time, but it can be easy to forget and if the invitation is underneath a stack of bills that you avoid, even easier!

If people haven't responded to your invitation in a timely manner by your suggested return date, a polite email or phone call to inquire about the return of the RSVP is perfectly acceptable. Don't go hard, be nice but also just reiterate that you'd love them to attend but are needing to confirm numbers, so would appreciate their response.

BRIDECHILLA STEPS

> **The less complicated and classic the invitation, the more value for money they will be.**
> **Save money by creating a wedding website page that includes details, instructions and maps.**
> **Think about the formality of the invitation and what message you want it to convey.**
> **Work backward with your time line of events to determine when guests need to know this information.**

if you fail to plan,
you plan to fail

A Bridechilla is a bride who believes love is all you need, but that a complementary color scheme is cool too.

Bridechilla Caitlín

Main Event : The Ceremony

IRONICALLY, ONE OF THE MOST NEGLECTED AREAS in wedding planning is the actual wedding itself: the ceremony, where the magic happens. For all the hullaballoo that we go through planning weddings, you'd be surprised at how many couples neglect to focus on the details of the ceremony.

THE REASON YOU'RE PLANNING THIS EVENT IN THE FIRST PLACE

It can be daunting to think about standing in front of a crowd of people, making declarations of love, especially for people who are introverted or aren't that confident when it comes to public speaking. But it doesn't have to be challenging for you. With a little preparation and forethought, you can create an emotional ceremony that truly reflects who you are as a couple. Including humor and light-hearted moments will add a personal touch too.

Rich and I chose to have a civil ceremony and worked with our wonderful friend and celebrant Vanessa on personalizing our wedding vows. She gave us a number of great options for how to incorporate our personal story into our vows. She asked a lot of questions about how we met, what makes us laugh, and how being in each other's lives has changed us. With her guidance and very handy worksheets and questionnaires, we were able to create a memorable ceremony that included some fun personal stories and incorporated what we really wanted to say to each other on this very important day.

The matter of incorporating faith and religion into your service might be a clear-cut decision for you. No matter who will be your celebrant, minister or registrant, make sure you take the time to work with them to make your wedding vows as personal and intimate as possible. When it comes to religion and including religious aspects and details into your wedding service, do what is important to you, not what you feel obliged to do. If your faith is a part of your life, great, include it in your wedding day. If you are an atheist but your parents want you to get married in a church, I encourage you to have that conversation early on.

Perhaps this isn't a big compromise for you, but more and more I am meeting couples who are stepping away from full religious services and adding snippets of tradition and readings into their ceremony. This is also a good compromise for mixed-faith marriages when choosing one or the other could cause rifts or problems.

When it comes to selecting a venue for your wedding ceremony, sometimes it can be challenging to juggle availability of a reception venue with the availability of a ceremony venue (if they are separate locations). Which is more important to you? If one isn't available, do you change the other location? You might want to consider the following things before locking in the details of your ceremony and officiant/minister/rabbi:

- If you are marrying in a church or synagogue, is there any pre-wedding coun-seling required?
- What is the fee and what does that include?
- Can you meet them in advance for a rehearsal?
- An obvious first question for an officiant – are they licensed to perform your marriage service?
- Can you write your own vows? Often church services are not very flexible, while civil ceremonies are largely your call, except for the mandatory legal declarations.
- Are there dress requirements for guests in the venue?
- How early is the venue/location available for decoration?
- Do you need to pack anything up after the ceremony?
- Do you need to hire additional microphones or PA equipment?
- If it is to be held outside, is there a rainy day contingency plan?

GETTING HITCHED OVERSEAS

If you are considering a destination wedding, investigate the legalities and validity of the marriage license and whether you will be considered legally married in your home country.

Some countries require you to apply for a marriage license up to a month be-fore the wedding, which is often an impossible task. A solution is to have a town hall service to legalize your marriage locally, and a civil "for show" ceremony at the destination. If you are eloping, talk to a wedding coordinator at your destination who should have the information regarding timing for license applications.

In our wedding planning and service, how we choose to acknowledge and honor someone who was close to us who has died is a personal and sometimes challenging decision.

First, remember that you don't have to do anything. If the emotions are raw, if you feel that it will be too much to include, then pay your respects in a way that suits you. Finding a balance between acknowledging your loved one while keeping the mood optimistic and joyful can be tricky, especially if their passing is recent.

Of course, everyone's situations are unique. How you choose to honor them is entirely dependent on what you are comfortable with. It doesn't have to be a public declaration, especially if you feel that this will affect you in a way that will possibly take away from the happiness of the day.

Personal gestures such as wearing an item of jewelry that was theirs, or something that they gifted to you can be a modest way to keep them close on the day. I wore my mother's watch (I wear it every day), and for me, it was a simple gesture that ensured that a 'piece' of her was with me all day and in our photographs. We also added a short but poignant acknowledgement in our wedding service of our loved ones who had passed away. It wasn't overly sentimental but it was important for us to mention how much we would have loved our grandmothers and my mother to be there to share our celebration.

There are other ways to share the memory of a relative or friend. You can light a candle in their honor, or some people like to leave an empty seat in the front row for a missing parent or relative. A table featuring photographs of family members who have passed away can also be a lovely gesture and of course music can be a wonderful way to remember people; perhaps include their favorite song or a piece of music that reminds you of them.

Whatever you choose to do, whether it is a private gesture or a public declaration, make sure that if fits with what you want the day to be about, being happy and in love – because surely whoever is no longer with you would wish that the most for you.

When it comes to the content of the ceremony, what you want to say to the person you are going to marry, it can sometimes be hard to find words that you are comfortable expressing in front of a large group of people. Some people may believe it's just easier to use a script because they are concerned with being overly emotional or getting caught up in their feels.

I think that's a real shame. What other time will we stand in front of the most special and important people in our lives and be truly honest about committing to another person, the person that we love and respect? The person that puts up with our shit and we put up with theirs. I am probably the least smooshy person on the planet, and I was concerned with not making our wedding ceremony too soppy because that's just not who we are as a couple. That's not to say we didn't add a bunch of romantic, personal and funny mementos of our love and relationship to our wedding ceremony. We avoided stock standard readings, and instead chose to include pieces by Woody Allen and Jerry Seinfeld that were both humorous and relevant to us.

ADDING PERSONALITY TO YOUR WEDDING VOWS

"To honor and obey" and "until death do us part" can be a bit of a yawn. Who talks like that? Add readings that are meaningful to you; ditch the stuffiness and invite friends and family members to contribute. Some movie and TV quotes might do the trick:

> I will never leave you. That's a promise. (Ripley, *Aliens*)

> It seems to me that the best relationships, the ones that last, are frequently the ones that are rooted in friendship. You know, one day you look at the person, and you see something more than you did the night before. Like a switch has been flicked somewhere. And the person who was just a friend is...suddenly the only person you can ever imagine yourself with. (Dana Scully, *The X Files*)

> When I'm around you, I kind of feel like I'm on drugs. Not that I do drugs. Unless you do drugs, in which case I do them all the time. (Scott, *Scott Pilgrim vs The World*)

> I love you.
> I know. (Han to Leia (AND Leia to Han), *Star Wars* (derr))

> We are all a little weird and life's a little weird, and when we find someone whose weirdness is compatible with ours, we join up with them and fall in mutual weirdness and call it love. (Robert Fulghum)

> Now join your hands, and with your hands your hearts. (William Shakespeare, *Henry VI*)

Whatever you do, take the time to work together to write meaningful words – don't leave this until the last minute. This is important. This is what it is all about. This is what people will remember.

> **Start thinking about your ceremony NOW!**
> **How can you make your wedding service really you, with readings and anecdotes that are meaningful to you.**
> **Make sure you connect with the person who is marrying you – they're pretty important to your day!**

A Bridechilla gives herself permission to have the day that she and her partner want, not what people expect.
She accepts and is enthusiastic about the ideas of others, even if they don't fit with the wedding she is planning – because she knows that there is more than one way to plan a wedding.

Wedding Decor, Flowers & DIY

FLOWERS ARE MARVELOUS, especially at weddings, but the cost of flowers can quickly turn your floral centerpiece dreams into nightmares. I think florists are very clever. I admire their skills greatly, and when I become a Real Housewife I am looking forward to having my own personal florist, who prepares weekly blooms for each room of the house, depending on my mood and scent needs.

At our wedding, we didn't allocate much of the budget for flowers. In fact, we spent $250 on flowers for our whole wedding. They weren't plastic and were not purchased from a supermarket or convenience store (all of which are viable options by the way).

We budgeted $300, so we were stoked we came in under budget. We aren't big flower people, we had a venue that had a lot of personality on its own, and we realized having lots of gorgeous flowers were completely out of our price range.

We found a local florist who proposed that we use Australian natives for my bouquet, the groomsmen boutonniere, and my bridesmaids' corsages. They were in season and suited our theme and style of my dress to a tee. They also agreed to supply us with yellow tulips (also in season) in bunches that we separated ourselves and placed in glass jars on each table at our reception. They were inexpensive and minimalistic, which suited us and our venue!

CHOOSING IN-SEASON FLOWERS WILL HELP YOU SAVE

When selecting wedding flowers (if you want flowers at all), it's a smart idea to choose blooms that are in season as they will potentially be less expensive and, most importantly, readily available. You might be surprised how many flowers in florists are flown in from all over the world, which can be very costly and not great for the environment. Speak with your florist about what is in season and work backwards from there.

Flowers such as gerberas, daisies, carnations, and chrysanthemums, in comparison to roses and orchids, are usually very reasonably priced. Choose irises, violets, daffodils, and tulips in spring. Lilies are plentiful and most affordable in the summer months. Roses and orchids are usually quite pricey despite the fact that they are widely available throughout the year.

BUY WHOLESALE

Flower wholesalers can save you money on your wedding day flower cost, but you need to do your research and know exactly what you want and then carefully consider the time and skills required to arrange flowers. If you are planning to visit a local flower market, be willing to get up early and follow their rules. Many flower markets now restrict entrance to business owners only and require ID, so if you are game to buy wholesale check with the entrance and purchase restrictions before getting your hopes up and again consider the time and skills that are needed to care for and arrange flowers in the lead up to your wedding.

LEARN THE LINGO: BUNCHES AND COUNTS

If you are exploring the DIY floral route, getting your flower lingo down is important. Wholesale flowers are almost always packaged by the grower in bunches. The bunch might be wrapped in a cellophane sleeve or tied together. Each variety tends to have a standard stem count per bunch, but there could be variations by the grower. Most wholesale flowers are cut and shipped before they have fully bloomed, so timing your purchase is also a bit of an art. This is information that florists have and, ultimately, like some DIY options that appear to be less expensive initially, having a trained expert that can manage the process can often be more beneficial than managing it yourself.

If visiting a wholesale market isn't in your plans, but you would still like to buy wholesale, then Bridechilla favorite Blooms By The Box offers fresh flowers at wholesale prices, shipped overnight to your venue. You get total creative control over the final look, and they offer some helpful tutorials that simplify the process of putting together centerpieces, bouquets, and other arrangements. Blooms By The Box also has flower packs that come with complimentary flower styles and colors, so you know you're getting a cohesive look for your event.

Local farmers' markets are also a good point of contact to speak with growers directly. Get there early and be prepared to travel to their farm or place of business to collect your order. Please note that you are buying raw, unarranged flowers so if you want fancy arrangements, flower crowns, bouquets, and center-pieces, someone is going to have to work hard to make that happen. Floristry is a skill and not something I would advise you to just try and figure out. The last thing you want to be doing on the morning of your wedding is having a flower freak out.

BUYING FROM A CHAIN

Big supermarkets and chains can mean substantial savings, but also your choice and personal service are limited. Although there's nothing quaint about saying, "We got our flowers at Costco," some of their packages are great value. They work with in-season flowers and there are dozens of options available. They're not the most dynamic arrangements but I have seen lots of very lovely weddings that have used Costco flowers, and the guests were none the wiser

SUPPORTING SMALLER LOCAL FLORISTS

In total contrast to the likes of Costco, I also encourage you to make friends with smaller, independent florists, as we did. Being open about your budget from the first meeting will help you establish realistic flower goals. It's not worth asking them to quote for a floral wall that you've seen on Instagram when you don't have a $50,000 budget for florals. Like many Bridechilla wedding planning decisions, compromising will get you far. If you want an elaborate bouquet, perhaps cut out the floral centerpieces or reception decorations. Even better, reuse flowers by moving them from your ceremony location to the reception, something a wedding coordinator can easily do. Also, when buying from a florist, you may be able to eliminate the delivery fee by picking up the flowers and decorations yourself (or assigning a member of the wedding party or coordinator to be in charge of this). By doing this though, the florist won't be on hand for set up, so be sure to have a plan and know what you are doing. Some questions you should consider asking your florist:

- Is there a delivery or on site set up fee?
- What time will the flowers (and florist) be arriving?
- If the flowers you choose aren't available on the day, does the florist pick the substitute or do you?
- Will they collect any rental items, vases, etc., after the wedding?
- Do they have another wedding booked on the day of your wedding?
- If you are picking up the flowers before your wedding, is there anything special you need to do to keep them fresh and alive?

BOUQUETS, BOUTONNIÈRES AND CENTERPIECES

Flowers are here today, dead tomorrow. Granted, they look pretty and smell nice, but they don't need to be everywhere, being clutched by everyone. Larger blooms like hydrangeas, lilies, rhododendrons, and peonies are beautiful and bold, take up more room and can cut down on cost. Also, consider using filler leaves, ferns, hydrangea leaves, limonium, and solidagos to add volume and complement floral arrangements.

Bridesmaids don't necessarily need individual bouquets, instead, pin one beautiful blossom on each of your attendants; a lady boutonnière or even an old school wrist corsage. This is a much more inexpensive option and this way the flowers have become part of their outfit and not left on a table in the bathrooms after an hour. For groomsmen, boutonnières look fabulous, and if they aren't wearing matching suits or outfits, this small detail can tie their look together.

TABLE FLOWERS AND CENTERPIECES

You don't need a massive floral centerpiece to make the table gorgeous. In fact, you don't need flowers on the table at all. If you are keen on having some "living" centerpiece but can't afford a full floral arrangement, then visit your local garden center or nursery and buy several trays of annuals or perennials that match your color scheme. You could also choose herbs, like oregano, basil and tarragon, which will give any setting an organic feel; I guarantee they will be whipped up by the guests to take home at the end of the day.

Instead of elaborate floral centerpieces that are filled with blooms, consider using small vases or vintage jars and fill them with a few flower stems. We chose yellow tulips for our wedding, which were compact, colorful, and neat. We purchased five bunches from the florist for 15 dollars each and asked the florist ahead of time when the flowers would bloom. This worked perfectly because we picked up our flowers the day before the wedding and they matured and blossomed overnight.

Ripe fruits are said to symbolize abundance and fertility; they're also yummy, cheap, and colorful. Tomatoes look beautiful and enticing in a rustic Italian display. You could include green or red apples, peaches, vibrant lemons or limes, grapes or pomegranates; stack them in cases, spray paint them, stick name cards in them – experiment to your heart's content.

Candles create an air of romanticism and come in all shapes and sizes. Gather different sized candles on vintage plates or trays. Sit them in vases surrounded by pebbles, sand, whatever you like. You can buy the pebbles and pillar candles from dollar shops, Target or Kmart. While you are shopping at these discount stores, you can also look for hurricane vases and clear pillar vases, which also look great with candles placed inside (especially if your venue will not allow open flames without a cover, which is most venues). Pet stores and nurseries sell pebbles in a variety of colors and textures (for fish tanks and fountains).

DON'T THROW AWAY YOUR WEDDING FLOWERS

Flowers are beautiful, so why not let someone else enjoy the beauty of your wedding flowers when you are off whooping it up on honeymoon? I am talking about the idea that you can recycle your flowers by donating them to hospices, hospitals and old folks' homes. It's a basic process, there are many charities and organizations that will come to your venue and collect them after the wedding. You'll never have to do anything out of your schedule, and often a lot of hotels and event companies will be involved with the charity as well.

Ask your wedding planner or venue if they are connected with one of these charities or organizations, and if they aren't, ask why not and what the hell they do with the flowers from all the functions they hold?! Can you imagine someone's nanna being able to have fresh flowers in her room, or terminally ill people in a hospice having lovely flowers? How nice is it to think that you can pass on these beautiful floral arrangements that you've had at your wedding and know that they will bring a bit of joy into other people's lives. That is the ultimate Bridechilla & Groomchilla move.

I also suggest you look into bloomrent.com, a company who will help you share and reuse your wedding flowers. They work directly with florists, and boast a big list of partners on their website. You get the quote, hire the florist and do all the stuff that you would normally do when having floral arrangements designed for your wedding. The florist then sees there is someone else in your neighborhood that would like to use the flowers after you. They can be redesigned and reused the next day. You can have a centerpiece that perhaps is being pulled apart and then put together the next day for a baby shower, or for a corporate event. You can negotiate a better price because the flowers aren't going to go to waste and they will be enjoyed by another group of people.

DIY AND DECOR

I freaking love crafts. I love painting stuff, getting my hands sticky with glue and look out if I get my hands on some fancy scissors...however, as much as I like getting heavily involved in a DIY task, I also know my limits.

Being a Bridechilla requires balance and knowing when to commit to a task and when to off-load it to someone else. Don't be a DIY hero if DIYing things is your worst nightmare. Pick projects that are pleasurable and you find worthy of committing your precious time to. If you want the DIY look but don't want to buy all the stuff and learn the skills, support an artist or supplier on Etsy or hire a skilled person on thumbtack.com or Fiverr.com to get the job done. Don't believe the hype, often DIY isn't cheaper. Unless you already have the tools and supplies it can really add up, particularly when you add your time to the bill. Pick your DIY battles. Don't get stressed about silly things, especially last-minute projects and details that won't make or break your wedding day.

If you are up for a DIY challenge, may I suggest you do one project at a time and not overcommit yourself? Pick the projects that are achievable and aren't too costly. DIY can look easy – sew this, print that, papier-mâché 678 balloons – but seven hours and two bottles of wine later you just want to go to bed. I found a website that suggested you make your own cocktail umbrellas. Really? Are you on crafting crack? Who has the time? How about you go to the supermarket and buy a pack of 100 for $3.99. Pick your battles. This one may not be worth the time nor the effort.

ADDING A PERSONAL TOUCH

It's nice to add a personalized touch to your venue with decorations, tableware, and flowers. Locations like museums and vineyards may need less adornment due to the nature of the venue. Before you go out and buy anything, speak to your venue manager or coordinator to see if they have any decorations, such as candles, lanterns, vases or lights, that you could use for free or hire at a small cost. It's always better to borrow than buy, both for your budget and the environment.

Decorative items do not have to be purchased from a home goods shop, in fact, it's best to avoid them all together. Scope out alternative stores, use Amazon, dollar stores, Michaels, hardware stores, post offices, and discount emporiums. When looking for decorative items, pick versatile materials, things that you can use for a number of wedding-related projects. Recycle when you can and change the way you look at household items; they can be transformed into the star of the show with a little bit of DIY magic if you are inspired.

CUT THE FAT AND THE FROOF

In my opinion, chair sashes and covers are over. In fact, one of *The Bridechilla Podcast*'s mottos is FUCK CHAIR COVERS! As well as being a literal message, it is also metaphorical. Chair covers are the item that I would first lose if you were looking to save money and you don't want big, shiny, elasticized lycra chair condoms ruining your wedding.

I am very passionate about this.

They are awful.

The worst.

A lot of venues insist on you renting them because they only supply plastic chairs. Take a look before you commit. Worst comes to the worst, spend the money that you would have spent hiring the chair condoms and hire some nicer looking chairs instead. A neat folding wooden chair (natural wood, black or white) looks far less fussy and is cheaper to hire. They can be personalized with a band of vintage material or small buntings, and they come with a cushion. If bows are your thing, go for it, but otherwise ditch them. In addition to the dining tables, you may want to decorate other extra tables such as the cake table, guest book (if you are having one) and gift table. You could try using the same tablecloths and motifs as the main reception area, or if in doubt, tone it down and use a plain white tablecloth.

SUSTAINABLE WEDDING PLANNING

Over the past five years of producing *The Bridechilla Podcast* one ongoing theme that I am particularly drawn to is the amount of waste that an event like a wedding can create. We are encouraged to invest in single-use items, from dresses to decorations, that often end up in landfill after sitting in a cupboard or garage.

Being mindful of your wedding's carbon footprint is not only a positive step for the environment, it can also save you money and give you that lovely, "I have done something good" smug feeling.

Planning a sustainable wedding doesn't mean that your guests will be sitting on straw bales and everything came from goodwill – although both of those options sound totally rad if you don't suffer from allergies and have an eye for a bargain!

Sustainability is about being mindful of waste, thinking about the item's usefulness (and re-usefulness) and not buying a bunch of plastic tat that will never be used again or thrown in the trash ten minutes after your guests get home (see my rant about favors later in this chapter).

Just like connecting with vendors who share your values, e.g. are LGBTQ friendly, finding vendors who are environmentally and socially responsible is also something that I encourage. For example, seek out caterers who are focused on reducing food waste and perhaps donate their leftover food to charity or are focused on reducing their use of factory-farmed meats and dairy. Hire a florist who works with bloomrent.com or similar floral re-use organizations, or work with a planner who is sustainably minded and is open to renting instead of buying wherever possible.

To minimize waste at your wedding, little steps can make a big difference. Reduce disposable items like plastic cups, straws and tableware. Rent glassware and crockery that can be used again.

Join local online wedding sale groups to buy repurposed décor, attire, and other wedding items (we have a Bridechilla Buy and Sell Facebook group, you should totally join)

Consider going paper-free or at least reducing your paper usage by creating a wedding website and encouraging guests to RSVP and communicate online. Wedding printables such as menus and programs are often glanced at for two seconds by guests and put aside; reduce these items by creating one menu per table, or one big wedding program timeline that you can make into a sign.

Rent bridesmaids' outfits, suits, and even your wedding dress (see the chapter 'Bridechilla Style and Frocking up' for more information). Not only will this reduce waste but the cost per wear is remarkably reduced. Another option is to buy pre-loved attire from websites like stillwhite.com or check out charity stores that sell wedding attire.

Before buying a wedding related item, take a moment to Marie Kondo the shit out of it (Google her) and ask yourself, "Does this item bring me joy?" and, "Does it add value to my guests' (and your own) wedding experience?"

Although balloons and lanterns were the hot item a couple of years ago they are something that every sustainable wedding day can do without. Balloons, although colorful and pretty, are an abomination to the environment and often end up in the ocean or being eaten by unsuspecting birds or animals. Lanterns that are often ceremoniously lit and float up into the atmosphere at the end of the night have been reported to have started wildfires, and if they don't burn out they just become litter.

Ask your venue about recycling. Do they recycle cans and bottles used at their events? If not, why not?

Taking positive steps towards sustainability is become an easier choice for all of us and knowing that your wedding's carbon footprint is smaller and that you have done your best to make positive changes is a wonderful feeling.

DIY WITHOUT THE Y

If you want that DIY, home-crafted, kitsch, vintage, indie feel to your wedding but are completely lacking in any DIY skills, then like most wedding related things, you can buy them and take the credit. Fake DIY is easy. Get someone else to package your almonds, or sew buntings or hand design your invitations. There is an abundance of crafty websites out there that will connect you with such people.

Etsy is a world of wedding suppliers, handmade items and accessories, uniquely wonderful decorations, clothing, jewelry, photo booth supplies – you name it, Etsy's got it. I love Etsy because you can find someone down the road who has a penchant for illustration and calligraphy to hand write your place cards, or locate an avid and talented knitter on the other side of the world to create specialized bespoke boleros for your bridesmaids. With millions of listed items, you will find what you're looking for, and without a shop front many artisans have items at very reasonable prices. I can get lost on Etsy, spend hours "favoriting" gloves and hats and stamps. It's a time-suck, so make sure you do it at work.

FAVORS

Okay. Let's pause a moment and think. Let's be sensible. I've been to a lot of weddings and there's no nice way to say this, but I've received a lot – a lot – of crappy, forgettable favors and gifts that I know probably cost the couple a ton and that I promptly threw away or left in a hotel room. I don't give a shit about favors. Truly. I could not care less.

Favors are something that started as a nice, inexpensive tradition. Traditionally referred to as bomboniere, they were a box containing "bonbons" (candies) given by hosts to their guests on special occasions such as bar and bat mitzvahs, weddings, baptisms, first communions or confirmations. They usually include Jordan almonds, known in Italian as confetti. Five sugared almonds symbolize health, wealth, happiness, fertility, and long life. That's it. Now we're giving people all sorts of shit, and it's costing us a lot of money.

If you're on a tight budget, this is the easiest thing (after chair covers because FUCK THEM) to get rid of. Many guests leave the reception without even taking their gifts home with them (wasteful on all levels). Who really needs a scented monogrammed candle or a key ring? A lot of the stuff that people give is mass-produced garbage and doesn't have any relevance to who they are, it's more of an obligation gift than anything.

If you are keen to give a small gift and want to add a personalized touch, bake some biscuits or sweets and repackage them with a copy of the recipe. Rather than spending up big on floral centerpieces, display your favors in the center of the table and allow your guests to take them home at the end of the night. A collection of small vases with individual flowers, vibrant lollipops, or jars filled with colorful chocolates will add zest to the table and serve two purposes.

A "living" favor such as a seedling in a jar or a packet of seeds to take home and plant can be nice. Again, these plants can also act as part of your wedding table decorations, adding variety, color, and life to each table and eliminating the need for centerpieces. Choose from a variety of plants such as lucky bamboo, succulents, cacti, yuccas, pot belly figs, and ponytails. All are hearty and hard to kill. That way people can go home and plant a little piece of you!*

Using a collection of recycled jars, fill them with soil and compost, sprinkle some seeds inside, place on a windowsill, and water whenever the soil is dry. Allow the flowers or plants plenty of time to grow. Keep the flowers and dirt in the jars and use as terrarium-style centerpieces or live-bouquets. Live plants bring a natural element to both indoor and outdoor weddings. It's also a wonderful way to save money, considering that a pack of 50 seeds is about $3.

DO YOU NEED A PINTERVENTION?

Pinterest, or as I call it, the-place-where-I-lost-five-months-of-my-life.com, is one of my favorite wedding and design resources. With hundreds of millions of users, there is an abundance of information, photographs, and best of all links back to the original source, so you don't have to spend 20 hours looking for that uncredited crystal belt you saw on an obscure design site.

As a Pinterest user, you can create your own online wedding pin board, borrow from others and be inspired. Pinterest can be completely overwhelming. There is so much to see and do and pin, it can take over your life.

A lot of the images featured on Pinterest, in particular from professional wedding websites, are styled shoots. These are editorial images that are used to show how you can decorate a venue or what a tablescape can look like. These are fantastic to use as inspiration, but you must be mindful that a lot of the time the set-up costs a bunch of money, and the designers have had a lot of time to work on the aesthetics that just may not be possible to emulate in a real-life environment.

It can be very easy to get carried away on Pinterest, so I suggest that instead of just pinning everything, you organize your boards into topics and areas that you truly want to gather inspiration for. Pinterest is also a clever way to communicate your design aesthetic and goals with your wedding planner, florist and other vendors that you're working with.

Creating secret Pinterest boards is a way to share those images with vendors and not necessarily have everything out on show if you don't want other people to see it. When you are sharing images with vendors, make sure that you only send a maximum of 10 to 20 images. A florist does not need to see 400 inspiration images. This probably will work against you rather than for you when it comes to really homing in on what you'd like to achieve. Be mindful of inspiration, and by that I mean be inspired, but not obsessed or infatuated with emulation.

> **Use local vendors.**
> **Use alternative decorations for table centerpieces and ceremony decorations.**
> **Use in-season flowers.**
> **Choose simple arrangements that you can create yourself.**
> **Visit flower markets and wholesalers but remember that floristry is an art and not something that you can just pick up overnight.**
> **If you are going to get your DIY on, do it with plenty of time. You don't want to be sewing napkins the night before the wedding.**
> **Choose projects that are worth your time. Don't hand paint 500 jars if you could buy them cheaper and no one is going to notice your handiwork.**
> **Utilize places like craft shops, discount suppliers, and Ikea.**
> **Themes can be subtle; you don't need to knock your guests over the head with it.**
> **Ask grandmas, mothers-in-law and crafty friends to help you out. If they're keen to help out, give them small tasks and jobs.**

* Check that your guests won't be traveling interstate or overseas because some jurisdictions will not allow plant or animal matter across their borders.

A Bridechilla is a bride who makes decisions based on actual reality instead of superstitions and peer pressure.

Bridechilla Brooke

A Piece of Cake

Mmmmmmm cake. Cakes are important, well, to me anyway. I love eating them, looking at them and thinking about them. Having a fabulous tasting and looking wedding cake (or cakes) doesn't have to break the cake bank. Wedding cakes can be labor intensive and costly, but they're also symbolic and sometimes one of the event's biggest focal points, especially if included on a dessert table. A wedding cake doesn't have to be a traditional tiered affair, you can have ten cakes, cheesecakes, donuts or if you aren't into cake (I am sad for you) you can even have a stack of cheese that looks like cake.

In a similar fashion to florists, shopping around, doing some cake tasting (YES!), and seeing what is on offer is a good first step. Generally, you can expect that the cost of a wedding cake will start around $3.00 per slice for traditionally decorated fruitcakes, but it can be up to $5.00. Depending on how many guests you are expecting, the average cost for a wedding cake will be about $300 to $700. Aside from the obvious, and dare I say risky, option of making the cake yourself, which can be an unnecessary stress so close to the day, there are plenty of other options to escape the costs of a traditional tiered wedding cake.

Consider how many people you are feeding. Be realistic about the wedding cake size that you really need. A four or five-tiered wedding cake can be flashy, but most couples only need two or three tiers at most. If you want to add extra tiers, consider opting for artificial tiers. Styrofoam can be decorated to look like a real tier and will also cost less (we did this, and no one knew).

You could also consider renting or buying a styrofoam show-cake from a baker (many do this for larger functions) and have the caterer serve your guests from sheet cakes that are plated in a back kitchen. Keeping the cake simple and avoiding fussy or handmade decorations will save you coin. If you choose a basic cake style instead of one with multiple flavors, icings, fillings or decorations, the price will reflect that. A cake is a cake right? There is nothing stopping you from going to a local bakery and ordering decorated cakes to create your own-tiered ensemble. Ask for a simple design or if you trust their skills and want something fancy, tell them to go for it. You can rent cake tiers from catering companies and bakeries for minimal cost, or you can make your own.

Once your guests are tucking in, they won't know the difference (or care). There's nothing more elegant than a simple white cake topped with fresh flowers. Fresh flowers are a wonderful way to decorate cakes and a great way to tie your theme together. Whether you have a matching bouquet or the same color scheme, fresh flowers look glamorous and are not hard to place on the cake yourself (Just check that they aren't toxic, or sprayed before putting them anywhere near the cake! For real. Please do this and communicate with your florist that the flowers will be used on food!).

Professional bakers and decorators, although often fabulously talented, have overheads such as rent and staffing costs that they work into the overall price. Unlike amateur photographers, amateur bakers are people I would consider hiring, especially if they are just starting out and haven't gone full-time yet with their passion. Instagram is a great way to find local bakers and cake decorators. When seeking amateur bakers always ask for references and examples of their past work. If you aren't completely sure of their skills, order a smaller test cake.

- Can they deliver?
- Has their kitchen been inspected by health and safety?
- Have they worked in different temperatures (this is particularly important for summer events)?
- Are they confident that they can deliver your order on time and on budget?
- Make sure you work together to produce a contract and get everything in writing.

Having a stand of cupcakes for a wedding cake is still massively popular, and there are plenty of bakers now specializing in making and decorating cupcakes. Cupcakes are cute and neat all stacked up in a tiered style. Cupcake stands are also readily available on eBay, and there is quite a good resale market as well. Most cupcake wedding cakes feature a smaller cake on the top tier, so the couple still have a cake to cut. Donuts are also a big winner. Some people create donut display boards (hooks that hold the donuts), and some bakeries are renting these boards for a small fee with a donut order. The other main benefit of cupcake wedding cakes and donut displays are that guests can serve themselves. I think one of the most annoying extra charges out there is the cake plating charge, or "cakeage". It can range from $3 to $8 a slice just to "plate the cake." Blerg.

DESSERT TABLES AND SELF-SERVE BARS

Dessert tables are my favorite #foodporn images to search for on Pinterest. I can look and drool at cakes and crazy donut walls and cupcakes all day. Instead of a grand tiered cake, why not create a dessert bar with pastries, smaller cakes, mousse, candy and cookies. You can ask your bridal party and extended family to bring along their favorite dessert. A dessert table not only looks scrumptious, it also gives your guests lots of options other than just a wedding cake. Again, check with your venue to make sure they aren't going to slug you with extra costs.

Dessert stations, where your guests can assemble their own sweet fantasies from brownies to sundaes, are also incredibly popular. You can hire a soft serve machine for a reasonable price then create your own selection of fresh fruit, sprinkles, fudges and condiments for decorations. Guests love to get involved, and this is a great way to personalize a dessert bar. When we got hitched, we had the now Instagram-famous Cake Ink create a marvelous three-tier cake and our friend who ran a boutique baking company made a selection of bite-sized treats to complete our dessert table. It was the focal point of the room and guests couldn't wait to dig in. We also included small takeaway boxes for guests to take home a selection of goodies instead of favors.

You could replace the cake entirely with a chocolate fountain! Chocolate fountains are a very popular addition. Chocolate fountain rental companies will supply everything you need to have a delicious chocolate or caramel fountain flowing throughout your wedding reception. Usually, fountains cost between $200 to $500 depending on the style you select and generally will include an operator to manage the fountain and clean-up (especially when drunk people put their faces under them...which is my dream).

BRIDECHILLA STEPS

> **The simpler the cake, the cheaper it's going to be.**
> **If you want a four-tiered cake but only need two tiers, use "fake cakes," saving money and food.**
> **Create a dessert bar with lots of variety and yummy cakes and additions.**
> **Calculate the cost per head for each piece of cake, it's an easy way to bring you back to reality when considering a $2,000 cake.**
> **Head to Pinterest and Instagram for cake inspiration and hunger pangs!**

Bridechillas are more concerned about respecting actual humans than subscribing to archaic forms of etiquette. And by "actual humans" I mean themselves, their partner, their family, their vendors – compromising with each based on their specific relationship to the bride/groom, rather than just following abstract rules.

Bridechilla Elizabeth

Speech Making & MCs

GIVING A SPEECH AT A WEDDING or event is a big deal, and for a lot of people, public speaking evokes feelings of extreme terror. I am reminded of this quote from Jerry Seinfeld:

> According to most studies, people's number one fear is public speaking. Number two is death. Death is number two. Does that sound right? This means to the average person, if you go to a funeral, you're better off in the casket than doing the eulogy.

It doesn't have to be this way! As a stand-up comedian, one of the most baffling comments I get, along with "Are you funny?" – seriously, how am I supposed to answer that? – is, "You are so brave getting up there!"

I speak on behalf of 98% of the stand-up comedians and performers I know who would not describe themselves as brave except perhaps when attempting to eat the food provided at seedy comedy venues. Now *that* is brave.

A lot of attention is placed on the success of the best man speech and just between you and me, I was slightly satisfied on one particular occasion watching a best man bomb after he told me that comedy comes naturally to him and he's going to ad-lib most of it because it sounds more natural that way. I didn't wish the awkward moments on him because he brought them on himself, although comedy karma rained down upon him because he once said, "It's a genetic fact that women can't be as funny as men." Here's a fact, I fucking hate this guy, and he doesn't understand what a genetic fact is. Scientist he ain't.

The point is, the dude thought he could wing it but the first step in being good at nearly anything, is practice and preparation, and public speaking is no exception.

You don't have to be an extrovert or professional big mouth like me to prepare a cracking speech. I want to give you some tips to ensure that your speech will instead be remembered for being witty, warm and genuine – just like you!

Bridechillas, I implore you to chuck out the awful patriarchal tradition of the silent woman at weddings. It's such bullshit. Why is it that only the groom speaks? If you have something to say, get up and make a speech. The irony is not lost on me that this is a day to celebrate the two of you and that most likely you've spent a good part of the year planning this shindig and yet you must not speak. It really irks me, nearly as much as being told by a numbnuts that my genetic make up means I am not as funny as those with a penis. I am Bridechilla. Hear me roar!

BE PREPARED

The success of smashing out a memorable speech (and stand-up comedy routine) is due to two things: preparation and authenticity. I know it is easier said than done, but it's way more effort to put on a front, to try to be something you are not, than getting up there and owning it as you. Without preparation, you may come off looking foolish or say something that will haunt you to the end of days, just like the ad-libbing best man who made so many cliché schoolboy errors.

PUSHING THE BOUNDARIES...TO A POINT

As a stand-up comedian it's fun to push the boundaries, to explore the taboo. However, a wedding isn't the place to discuss the groom's history of STDs, exes and divorce. Perhaps you're the maid of honor and feel deep down inside that the couple isn't "4eva." The wedding isn't the place to air these feelings, particularly after a couple of glasses of champagne courage. If you really feel strongly about sharing that opinion, do it before the wedding, loooong before the wedding.

Even jokes, like, "We didn't think you'd last," or, "We never really liked the bride (or groom)," or, "Although we really thought your last boyfriend was tops, we've warmed to the groom," are probably best kept under your hat. Sarcasm is fun, I love it, but often deep down these comments are true and possibly rather hurtful, so unless they're fun and lighthearted keep the criticisms cool and don't go too hard. It's a speech wishing the couple well, not a roast.

KICK THE NERVES

Nerves are a killer. Often people resort to booze to dull them. I can say in all my years of standing up and telling jokes to strangers I have never drank and talked.

Don't get me wrong, I love a tipple, but when I am on stage, I am at work. You don't drink at your desk – or do you?! I prefer to be fully in charge of my brain and mouth, knowing that I can cope with hecklers, dud microphones and whatever other challenges are thrown in my path. I'm not saying you have to be Sober Sally on the day, just don't get hammered before you get up there. You might think you're fun and hilarious tanked but that is not always the case. Breathing, although obvious for the continuation of life, is also an excellent nerve-buster and freak-out diminisher. Gentle breaths are best, just make sure they are not directly into the microphone or you'll sound like you're from a 1-900 number. Sometimes before I go on stage I like to say a little mantra to myself, "You can do this!" or, "Even though you didn't get into acting school, you're still an excellent performer!" Try not to let anyone else overhear you saying this though, and make sure the microphone is OFF. I cannot stress this last point enough. OFF!

WHAT DO YOU WANT TO ACHIEVE?

When you are writing the speech (months in advance because you have taken note of my first point, be prepared!), a delicate mix of sincerity and humor, possibly causing some mild face-palm moments but avoiding any post-speech cocktail fork stabbings, is ideal. I'm supposed to say go for heart over laughs, but really, laughs are what I want. Sweet, sweet laughs. The perfect speech is 90% laughs, 10% heart.

We once endured 25 minutes of the groom using his speech as a sort of verbal LinkedIn presentation, talking about how lucky the bride was to have him. It was gross. Think about your audience. It's family and friends. You are there to celebrate love and the coming together of two rad people. Save the sex stories for the bachelor and bachelorette parties. Grandma has only got a few years left, she doesn't need a detailed account of her grandson dry humping a pregnant stripper while wearing a moose costume, no matter how funny/tragic that is.

MASTER OF CEREMONIES

We recently attended my cousin Belinda's wedding in Hawaii. Belinda is Australian and she married the lovely Luke, who is American. Belinda and Luke asked me to be the Master of Ceremonies (MC) for their wedding, something that is often not included in U.S. weddings. In Australia and Britain, and I'm sure elsewhere, it is commonplace to invite a friend or family member to host the wedding instead of asking a DJ or someone you've never met to act as an MC. The role of an MC is to perform an introduction, lighten the crowd up a bit and introduce the speeches. What I really love about having someone who knows you host the wedding is that they add another level of personalization to your day that some-one who has never met you just can't achieve. I relished having that role on the day, and it meant so much to me that I could bring a little bit of our Australian traditions to their U.S.-based celebrations. The DJ, Mike, loved it because he just played his music. I know the work I put into preparing some talking points about key family members and the differences between Australians and Americans re-ally went down well too.

I've spoken a lot about this difference in our cultures on *The Bridechilla Pod-cast*, and have received a lot of positive feedback from my American listeners, who are keen to explore the option of having an MC. A lot of the time, people have relatives and friends who are vivacious, outgoing folk, who don't necessar-ily have pre-existing roles in the wedding party, but this opportunity to MC the wedding could be a perfect job for them. My main advice is, if you are choosing to go down this path, find someone who you trust to stay relatively sober, to be able to follow a schedule, and who knows you and your family, or who will at least do some research and be comfortable speaking in front of a group.

I have hosted weddings for my friends and family, and I see the role as an ex-tension of the wedding planner, in the sense that I work with the wedding planner to make sure that the day is running on time, that we're following the schedule. If things need to move faster or, for example, the sunset is approaching and photos need to be taken, then you can jump on the microphone and let everyone know what's going on. The role comes with responsibilities, so be mindful of choosing someone that will make you proud and also do a great job.

BRIDECHILLA STEPS

> **Finish the speech on a high; a nice anecdote from your friendship/relation-ship is always a winner.**
> **Be sure to make eye contact with the crowd and the couple. It really ups the ante.**
> **Practice the speech (lots!) and if you need notes, get it down to dot points, so you aren't just reading it.**
> **Focus on speaking slowly (we all race when we are nervous) and don't forget to raise a toast before you finish. Something simple like, "Here's a toast to love and laughter and happily ever after!" always goes down well.**

you can't make
everyone happy,
you are not donuts

A Bridechilla is someone who knows that she's planning a party first and foremost. A milestone to be sure, but a party nevertheless. Keeping that in perspective helps to stay calm and relaxed by realizing that it's her and her partner's party; they can do whatever they want (as their budget allows), and that any inevitable problems can be fixed with wit and patience.

Bridechilla Joan

Wedding Transport

IF YOUR CEREMONY and reception are at the same venue you get ten gold stars: First it's convenient, and second if you genuinely want to save money, you can do yourself a favor and skip right past any specialized wedding car services. If your ceremony and reception venues are in different places, then you will need a plan for how you and your guests will get from one place to the other.

Providing guest transportation isn't a deal breaker, in fact, most guests wouldn't expect transport to be included (unless you are away from civilization). But be conscious of guests' drunk driving and if you can offer other options to help them get home, do.

Our venue was an hour out of the city, along a highway and then down a dark bushy road. A cab ride to or from the venue would be at least $100. We were totally out of money at that stage, the budget was bare, but in the end, we came to a compromise. A few months before the wedding we asked our guests whether they would be interested in taking a bus, for a small fee, to the venue. It would pick them up and return them to a central location in Melbourne. We had about 30 responses of "yes please!" With that we hired a bus, asked a friend to collect $20 as people got on the bus, and then had them pay the driver. We would have loved to have offered a free bus ride for our guests, but we saw this compromise as a way to ensure that no one was driving when they shouldn't be. The journey also ended up being a nice way for people to get to know each other before they arrived at the wedding venue.

FLASHY CARS THAT NO ONE SEES

Arriving at your wedding in a flashy old vintage car that you paid $900 to hire for an hour but no one will see you in, to me, is a strange tradition. Cars are an expensive and often unnecessary addition to the wedding day bill. Unless the car is pulling up directly in front of your guests, no one is going to witness your grand arrival in your flashy, pricey car. I'm not suggesting that you turn up to the wedding in an old clapper, but looking at alternative options will be a guaranteed money saver. When it comes to limos, Jerry Seinfeld once again hits the nail on the head:

> You know what I never get with the limo? The tinted windows. Is that so people don't see you? Yeah, what a better way not to have people notice you than taking a thirty foot Cadillac with a TV antenna and a uniformed driver. How discreet. Nobody cares who's in the limo. You see a limo go by, you know it's either some rich jerk or fifty prom kids with $1.75 each.

Sorry limo lovers but limos are over – and so are Hummers. They have a high price tag due to all the unnecessary extras that come with them. Do you really need an eight-passenger limo with a television, flashing lights, full sound systems with subwoofers for just yourself and your bridal party?

Chauffeurs, private car services, and sleek black sedans are far more affordable and are unassuming and classic. You can also look into a classic car club in your area and see if you can hire one of their members to drive you and your bridal party. You can also rent an older car, like a Mustang or a convertible and drive yourselves, or simply use your own car. No one is going to remember the car; it's the person in it that counts!

USE UBER AND LYFT AS WEDDING CARS

The shared economy is a marvelous thing. Uber and Lyft have jumped on board the wedding train (apologies for the mixed metaphors) and are offering a number of options for you and your guests if you are getting married where their services are available.

Before you start the, "Hey Aleisha, I don't want to be picked up by some Bluetooth-wearing guy who plays talkback radio too loudly and drives his Prius like it's a getaway car to my wedding"—just relax. Lyft Lux and Uber Lux both offer snazzy cars that are specifically for transporting people to events like weddings and business meetings.

Although you can't "book" a car in advance, if you order with enough lead time - which will be easier if you are getting married in a place like a city or large metro area - the car will get you there just fine.

For transporting your guests, both Uber and Lyft have special events pages where you can create personalized discount codes for your guests to use. You can add credit to the event page to help guests pay for their trips. Guests that want to participate simply download the Uber or Lyft app, then they can use your personalized promo code to receive a discount. For new rideshare users, another option is to give them your personal referral discount code (which you can create within both apps), and they receive a discount, and you receive credit after they ride. Winner!

BRIDECHILLA STEPS

> **If no one is going to see you in the fancy car, ditch it.**
> **Check overtime costs with the chauffeur company in case there are unplanned delays.**
> **If you have a non-drinking generous friend, ask them to be your wedding day driver.**
> **If you must have a "fancy car", use it for the arrival or departure only.**

A Bridechilla is someone who gets that their wedding day is about marrying their bestie and celebrating their love and journey together surrounded by the people they care about most. They know that the cake, the music, the food and every wedding thingamajig in between (if they're not eloping) isn't about pleasing their families or their guests – it's about infusing their style and flavor into their love party!

Bridechilla Daniela

Gifts, Registries & Honeymoon

THE ETIQUETTE OF GIFTING and registries has evolved quickly in recent times with new companies popping up every day whose primary focus is helping you get the gifts that you need/want, making it easier for your guests to purchase those gifts, and helping you avoid the inevitable selections of George Forman Grills and foot spas (why!?).

The easiest way to avoid unwanted gifts is by creating a gift registry or wedding list. Traditionally, couples choose a retailer, usually a department or homewares store, and then create a list of desired items that they then share with guests. This way, no two people buy the same gift.

There has been a recent trend towards gift list services that allow couples to add almost anything to their gift list. Zola.com is a great example. Zola is an all-in-one wedding registry where you can register for the things that you need and want, as well as experiences, cash funds, and honeymoon funds. They also offer a group gifting option that allows your guests to make contributions towards higher-priced wedding gifts and you can even add products from other stores to your wedding registry. When your wedding is done, they let you pick exactly when and where you want your gifts to ship so you won't be bombarded with unexpected boxes.

Most registry companies will also supply you with registry cards to include in your invitations, and wedding websites also have other distribution methods for guests who are not computer savvy. Although wishing wells (where people post envelopes of money as gifts into the well) are still popular, some couples feel uncomfortable asking directly for money as a gift. With registries, you can choose for contributions to go towards something you really need. I have friends who purchased their first home together before the wedding and instead of gifts asked guests to contribute to their kitchen renovation. After completion, they had a big party to thank everyone. It was fabulous, and knowing that we helped them create something that they really loved was thanks enough.

The average contribution to gift registries is between $85 and $150 per person. If you have 100 people attending your wedding and 75 people contribute $70, you will have $5,250 in your registry account. That would pay for an amazing getaway or a whole bunch of great furniture.

HONEYMOONS

I regard traveling as one of life's joys. Rich and I work to travel. We always say that we are going to save money, but then a trip comes up, and we are gone (ahem, my money story is a classic example of this). I consider traveling to be about really seeing and experiencing a destination, not just going to a resort. Don't get me wrong, I love a cocktail and a pool, but my capacity for sitting and doing nothing maxes out after about two days. I encourage you to broaden your travel horizons and explore less traveled honeymoon destinations; step out of the Sandals package holidays and really go somewhere. The choice of accessible destinations continues to grow with exotic sites that are far from the popular, mainstream options. You can combine some clever hacks and fantastic deals to get your tropical vibes or adventure boots on, for a fraction of the cost of a "normal" honeymoon.

Although I would love to say that Rich and I travel in luxury, we don't. We love a bargain and "travel hack" as much as possible. Travel hacking is the art of collecting frequent flier points and miles to get free flights, hotels, tours and more. It can also involve using cashback websites, error fares and affiliate links. This may sound complicated but, in fact, it is easy peasy. Paying for your wedding expenses using a credit card (and paying it off!) is not only good practice for keeping a paper trail and covering yourself in case of any claims or overcharges. Choosing a credit card that helps you accrue points and travel miles can be a very worthy option when it comes to booking your honeymoon.

On our honeymoon, Rich and I took advantage of a special that American Express runs with their partner, The Small Luxury Hotels of the World. We joined their loyalty program (for free) and automatically received exclusive rates, complimentary breakfast, room upgrades and much more. The upgrades were the best! In Florence, when we got engaged, we booked with our American Express card and were upgraded from a standard room to a penthouse. We nearly lost our minds. It was very lucky, but paying with the card and asking for the upgrade meant that they were obliged to move us and at the time the only room they had was the penthouse – a win for us! We rarely travel without using some sort of deal. We aim to save at least 10-50% off hotels (plus earning free nights) whenever we book. It's a little fun, tight-ass challenge that I find rewarding. We have also achieved some great deals using priceline.com auctions and price matching websites, with free upgrades and extras that we would never have been offered if we hadn't searched. We always use cashback websites such as Rakuten. It is so simple, and once you start using it, I guarantee you won't want to make an online purchase without it. Rakuten offers a bunch of extra coupon codes that you can use in addition to the % off deals which are great for saving money on insurance, car rental, hotels, and flights. Check out thebridechilla.com/cashback to learn more and receive a special Bridechilla bonus!

Another favorite of ours is hotels.com. They have a handy rewards system: you collect 1 night for every night you stay at an eligible hotel. Once you have collected 10 nights, you'll get 1 free night at an eligible hotel (again, hello honeymoon). By combining these steps, you save, save, save. We also subscribe to a newsletter called Secret Flying, which posts daily updates for amazing error fares and hotel deals. There are plenty of other newsletters and clubs to join that can share these offers.

DISCOUNT VOUCHERS AND DEALS

Discount voucher sites such as groupon.com offer excellent deals on hotels, restaurants and accommodations. Again, forethought and planning are needed, but there are deals to be had. Always read the terms and conditions before buying the deal and check airfares and contact the hotels or resort to check availability. One snag with these vouchers is that they are often peak season deals so airfares can be very expensive. Check tripadvisor.com for reviews and photographs of the accommodation facilities.

Subscribe to travel deal websites and keep an eye out for partnership deals with airlines and accommodation companies with packages and special discounts. Travel sites like kayak.com allow you to search for flights based on factors that can significantly alter prices, such as the number of stops or time of day. By purchasing tickets for a red-eye or multi-stop flight, you can save hundreds on airfares. When dealing with travel agents, airlines and hotels, tell everyone that you are newlyweds. It can make you an instant VIP. Often hotels will gift you a bottle of champagne or a gift basket, and complimentary upgrades are also a possibility.

VRBO AND AIRBNB

One way to really live like locals is to combine a fabulous destination with the wonderful world of Airbnb and VRBO. Renting the holiday home or apartment of a local is ideal for getting out of the tourist parts of town and seeing the destination from the perspective of someone who lives there. It doesn't mean that you can't have luxury, in fact, some of the offerings on Airbnb and VRBO are far more affordable and luxurious than hotels. From stilt houses under the stars to penthouse apartments overlooking city skylines to fairy-lit tree houses in the woods, the options are endless.

BUDGET HONEYMOON IDEAS

If your wedding has drained the bank account, consider planning a mini-moon, a couple of nights away to decompress after your wedding and then save to go on a longer trip elsewhere down the track. This is a great way to extend your wedding vibes and really milk the "just married" treats! Some Bridechilla tips for short breaks on a budget:

- Work the cost of the honeymoon into your original budget.
- Honeymoon at home – spend some time on the couch and visit restaurants and local attractions that you've never gotten around to seeing.
- Use frequent flyer points to plan your great escape. Collect away and book ahead of time as airlines offer limited seats. They are often red-eye and early morning flights, but you can score some amazing deals.
- Ask friends and family if they have a holiday cottage, house or shack available to rent or borrow.
- Join a holiday home swap community online and arrange a house swap at home or overseas (plan ahead with this one). Homelink.org has been running since 1953 and represents home swappers in 27 countries, and with over 13,000 homes on the list you are sure to find somewhere fabulous. It's safe, and you could stay somewhere exotic that would otherwise be out of your price range.

BRIDECHILLA STEPS

> **If you plan to pay for the honeymoon, add it to your wedding budget.**
> **If you can't afford a honeymoon, plan for a big first anniversary trip.**
> **Collect and use frequent flyer or shopper deals.**
> **Use a gift registry to avoid receiving gifts you don't want or already have.**

no one regrets a holiday

To me being a Bridechilla is about being yourself and having a wedding that's a reflection of you and your OH. It's saying fuck it to the "shouldas".
It's about letting go of expectation and pressure from family, friends and the media and having an authentic self/ couple wedding.

Bridechilla Betty

The Truth About Wedding Night Sex

WE DID NOT HAVE SEX on our wedding night and I am totally fine with it. In fact, over the years I have started to wear it as a Bridechilla badge of honor, smashing yet another unrealistic expectation that after a day/night of partying (and months of preparation) that you will be somehow be at your most sexy and ready to return to your hotel room to a bed strewn with fresh rose petals and make sweet, sweet passionate love all night. Screw that. Here are the reasons we didn't have sex:

- We were freaking exhausted. Like, could-barely-remove-clothes exhausted.
- My sister- and brother-in-law were in the adjoining room and we could literally hear them turning over in bed and sniffing. Did we desire a family-based auditory audience? No thanks.
- We had about three hours before we had to be awake again to have breakfast with our people, then pack up and depart the venue.

I don't know about you but for me, sex is good when you feel like having it (always consensual; no contest there). I don't particularly want to have sex on a schedule or if I am not feeling the vibes. Nor should anyone, which is yet another reason why the obligatory wedding night shag shouldn't happen just because you think you should do it.

A few months ago, I posted a question on Reddit (the place where you can get honest answers to anything) asking users to share some details about their wedding night. The responses were honest, funny and surprising.

I think the topic of wedding day sex should be spoken about a lot more in a realistic light, so that's what we're going to do.

WHY THE PRESSURE?

The consummation of marriage – aka having sex on your wedding day – is another tradition that is steeped in details that are now meaningless in Western society. In the past, consummation was considered important because it was the act that proved the bride's virginity; the presence of blood was taken as definitive confirmation that the woman was indeed a virgin. People would come in post-sex and inspect the sheets and her bedclothes to prove the act had taken place and more importantly, that there was blood and the bride was pure. Oy.

Nowadays, most people aren't virgins when they get hitched. For the few that are virgins and decide to wait until their wedding night, of course, I can see the appeal of wedding night sex. Even though your first time can be sloppy and awkward, I would strongly advise going into the experience with reasonable expectations.

Continuing the "best day, greatest day, perfect day" messaging that we are regularly fed around how your wedding (and wedding night) are supposed to be, the expectation that when you hit the sheets you will have the "best night ever" can put a lot of pressure on couples, whether you are new to sex or not.

> We were both virgins and very excited to go for it. On our wedding night, we had a lot of fun trying, but he was worried about hurting me. At 2:00 a.m. we decided to take a break and go out for pancakes. We had a flight the next morning, the passengers behind us asked how many hours we had been married to settle a bet. I guess we looked like the newlyweds we were. That night we officially lost our virginity to each other. Good times. It's been 23 years. Still crazy about each other.

WHAT ARE YOUR EXPECTATIONS?

For Rich and I, whether we had sex or not on the evening of our wedding was not a deal breaker. Neither of us believed the marriage was to be cursed if we didn't, and we both agreed that obligation sex sounded pretty unsexy and that we'd far rather wait and actually enjoy it rather than just "get it done" for the sake of getting it done.

If it is important to you – and by no means am I begrudging you for wanting to have sex with your partner on this romantic and fun day – factor it in. And before you say, "Aleisha, I am not adding 'sex' to our wedding schedule," I simply mean, if sex is a must, if you feel like your wedding night isn't complete without having sex, then pace yourself with booze (you know your limits), consider when you might leave the party, and if you are tired or a little buzzed, don't put too much in the expectations box about the quality of the experience.

Talk with your partner about what you both imagine the evening to be. Will they be devastated if you don't have sex? Will you? Have realistic goals for the night. Be open to the prospect of wanting to stay on and party with your friends or going with the flow.

> It was important to my now-husband and he told me this before the wedding, so we didn't get too wasted at our reception, we left a bit earlier, booked a nice hotel room, and we had sex. It wasn't the best ever (the best was during the honeymoon!), but it was still very special doing it for the first time as husband and wife. Personally, I wouldn't have minded it either way, but because he said he wants that "first night" of husband and wife, we did it and it was still pretty amazing, have no regrets going to a nice hotel, spending some time with my new husband and being intimate.

If you know that perhaps you want to party the night away and you may not hit the sheets until dawn, you could do what this couple did and schedule some time to sneak off to their room. As long as you don't have your mother-in-law knocking down the door wondering why the hell you have gone missing from your own wedding, this sounds like a fun diversion!

> We had read that most couples are too tired so we vowed to make it happen – but we also didn't want to compromise on our fun! So obviously that meant getting creative. We snuck away between the ceremony and reception to our room and made it happen, it was quick and no one climaxed and there was a lot of dress in the way, but it was so much fun and just a little naughty, so us. We then partied the night away and eventually collapsed in a heap to sleep guilt free. It did make it easier that we had a destination wedding and everything was right there, but we would have made it happen no matter what.

> My husband and I did. We had a Sunday evening reception that ended at 9pm, so we weren't completely exhausted at the end. After the reception ended, we had a mini after party at the hotel's bar with those who were staying there that night. Once we got back to our room, we made good use of the jacuzzi tub in the bridal suite and got it on! 10/10 for actually having sex when we thought we'd be too tired.

> That night after our reception was over, we came back to our room and drank the bottle of champagne they left in our room for us and talked about life out on the deck until 5am. That moment was better than the sex we could've been having. We talked about our hopes and dreams, goals, and reflected on our special day. I couldn't have asked for a better end to it all.

> Lol nope. We brought a bottle of scotch and some cake back to the hotel room, watched *Legion* on a laptop, and passed out. It was awesome.

NOT HAVING SEX IS NOT FAILING

Whether you end up having sex or not on your wedding night, I can assure you, as someone who has been happily married and boning for many years, that it won't make or break your marriage.

Remove the pressure from yourselves to have the best sex of your lives (or even have sex at all) on your wedding night, especially if you just aren't feeling it. Be yourselves and have fun and remember you have years ahead of you to shag all over the place whenever you want.

BRIDECHILLA STEPS

> **Have sex on your wedding night - or don't! It really doesn't matter.**

you have as many hours
in a day as Beyoncé

To me, being a Bridechilla is about creating a day that is what you and your fiancé actually want. It's about enjoying the process, rather than stressing. It's not worrying what others think (whilst still being considerate). It is thinking outside the box, always having perspective that this is ONE DAY and reminding ourselves that no-one cares as much about this day as we do, so chill out.

Also: fuck chair covers. Duh.

Bridechilla Jess

Go Forth & Conquer!

WELL, MY DEAR WEDDING PLANNING Jedi Bridechillas and Groomchillas, we have reached the end of the book. My hope is that you can return to it during your wedding planning to reinstate chill and calm in times of potential insanity. Whether this is your first wedding or your third, whether you're marrying a boy or a girl, whether it's a big event or small, your wedding will be the most fantastic event because YOU planned it and you are marrying your special other person.

Being a Bridechilla is about maintaining focus and not being diverted by details and opinions that don't matter to you or your guests. Fuck chair covers and all the extra things we get distracted by but ultimately mean nothing. You can't control other people or their behavior and sometimes the silliness of it all, the things that people care about and make a big deal about, is just laughable. If someone has a ridiculous piece of advice that makes you want to punch a wall, don't get mad – deflect with humor, deflect with laughter, deflect with wine.

Welcome the generosity and love of family and friends; they want to help you wherever they can. But also don't feel obliged to do things their way because you think it's the "right thing to do." Find a balance. Find your voice and enjoy yourself. Don't panic, breathe, and be damn proud of yourselves for pulling this whole day together!

I'd love to meet you in the Bridechilla Community, our private Bridechilla Facebook Group, and be sure to subscribe to *The Bridechilla Podcast* and visit thebridechilla.com to learn more about complete Bridechilla domination!

Happy days and much love
Aleisha
x

● Remember when it's all done to write thank you notes to your guests! ●

The Maidchilla
Manual

GIVE YOUR BRIDESMAIDS THE GIFT OF CHILL

A Maidchilla is a chilled Bridesmaid who isn't fazed by dress drama, WhatsApp ghosting and inane power struggles. The *Maidchilla Manual* is the ultimate bridesmaid guide (and gift!), taking them through all of the events leading up to the wedding, and providing calming mantras and solutions to any potential 'people problems' that may come their way. Help your bridesmaids help you by gifting them a copy of the *Maidchilla Manual*.

The *Maidchilla Manual* features:

> Checklists and timelines of all potential pre-wedding events
> Party inspiration for bachelorette/hens, bridal showers
> Guidance to help your bridesmaids get in the Maidchilla mindset
> Helpful questions and tips to ensure smooth communication
> Each *Maidchilla Manual* comes with a complimentary "Will You Be My Maidchilla?" gift card

The *Maidchilla Manual* will show you how to be a bad-ass Bridesmaid, ditch the drama and get shit done!

Visit **bridechillastore.com** to get your copy. **Happy Days!**

The Bridechilla
Field Guide

GET ORGANIZED LIKE A BOSS AND STAY FOCUSED ON WHAT MATTERS MOST!

Take the *Bridechilla Field Guide* with you wherever you go and keep track of all your plans and wedding details in one place. It's bullshit-free*, useful and fun. Its easy to follow format helps you decided which tasks are important to your planning and what can be thrown in the f*ck it bucket. Team it with the companion *Bridechilla Survival Guide* and you'll be on a fast track to wedding planning zen.

The *Bridechilla Field Guide* features:

> Helpful questions to ask all of your vendors
> Comprehensive (no-stress) wedding planning checklist
> Bridechilla wedding planning guidance to help you know what to do when
> Plenty of space for notes and keeping track of all your important wedding information

The *Bridechilla Field Guide* is the fill-out-able must-have for modern couples who want to organize like a boss and stay focused on what matters most.

* Disclaimer: Does not contain references to "perfection" or "the best day of your life".

Visit **bridechillastore.com** to get your copy. **Happy Days!**

The Wedding Day Emergency Kit

BE CHILL: BE PREPARED FOR ANY EVENTUALITY

No matter how prepared and organized you may be, be on the safe side and pack the compact and handy Bridechilla Wedding Day Emergency Kit. Being a Bridechilla is all about being prepared and ready to tackle any potential problem with calmness and chill. This wedding emergency pack is a discreet cosmetic bag and kit that contains helpful, travel-sized items that will guarantee to get you out of any last-minute preparation jams.

The Bridechilla Wedding Day Emergency Kit contains:

> Sewing kit
> Band-aid and blister pack
> Earring backs
> Bobby pins

> Comb and hairbrush
> Dental kit
> Vanity kit
> Double-sided tape

Complete with calming Bridechilla mantras and a delightful bag with two zip compartments for future use, the Bridechilla Wedding Day Emergency Kit is an ideal gift for brides and is a must-have item on your wedding planning to-do list!

Visit **bridechillastore.com** to get your copy. **Happy Days!**

The Bridechilla
Podcast

GIVE YOUR BRIDESMAIDS THE GIFT OF CHILL

Life's too short to be worrying about wedding favors, obligation guests, and bridesmaid dramas. *The Bridechilla Podcast* gives you practical guidance and support to help you plan a meaningful wedding celebration. Covering everything from planning timelines to mental health, family dynamics to body image, Bridechilla is bullshit-free and keeps it real.

Listen to *The Bridechilla Podcast*, the world's #1 wedding planning podcast that inspired the Bridechilla wedding planning guides. Join Bridechilla founder and host Aleisha as she interviews expert guests about making the process easier and have a laugh at the often complicated business of planning a wedding.

There are 400+ free episodes to download and listen to right now, including regular listener Q&A episodes. Search for and subscribe to *The Bridechilla Podcast* wherever you get your podcasts.

Visit **thebridechilla.com/podcast** to find out more. **Happy Days!**

ALEISHA MCCORMACK

Aleisha is an Australian comedian, podcaster and TV producer. She has worked as a writer and presenter for popular Australian comedy, panel and lifestyle programs, including Channel 10's *The Circle* and *The Project*.

Performing solo stand up comedy shows at international comedy festivals, Aleisha also toured the country with her one-woman show *How To Get Rich*, based on the adventures of meeting her husband Rich (they met on the internet and Aleisha flew across the world on a whim, from Melbourne to London, to meet him for the first time).

Rich and Aleisha got hitched in Melbourne in an intimate DIY wedding in 2012. Surprised by the level of A1 bullshit surrounding the wedding industry and additional pressure placed on couples to plan a "perfect day", Aleisha was inspired to start *The Bridechilla Podcast* to empower like-minded couples to plan their own wedding without losing their sanity.

Having produced hundreds of podcast episodes and built a community of free-thinking Bridechillas from all over the world, Aleisha is delighted and surprised that what she started has become a movement.

She resides in London with her current husband Rich, and her drink of choice is vodka, lime and soda. She's a reformed Nutella addict and her drunk party trick is doing the splits.

FUCK PERFECT

Bridechilla Founder Aleisha McCormack